I0468786

WINTER SEASON WITH NATURE

Landscape Scenes

Poetry-Photography

Author

Peggy Leyva Conley

Thank you for reading. In the event that you
Appreciate this book, please consider sharing the
Good word(s) by leaving a review, or connect with
the author.

All rights reserved. Aside from brief quotations for
Media coverage and reviews, no part of this book
may be reproduced or distributed in any form
without the author's permission. Thank you for
supporting authors and a diverse, creative culture
by purchasing this book and complying with
copyright laws.

Copyright © 2016 - Peggy Leyva-Conley
Poetry and Photography

All Rights Reserved

Printed in the United States of America

ISBN-13: 978-1530631858 (Createspace) paperback
ISBN-10: 1530631858

Table of Contents

About the Author

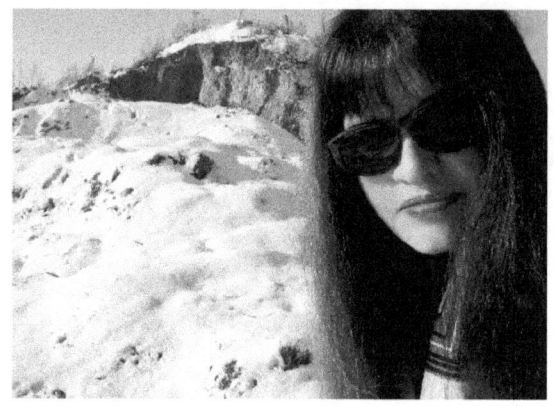

Peggy Leyva Conley was born in Hollister, California,
San Benito County on the Pacific Central Coastal
region bordering Monterey County. She has resided in
Hendersonville, Tennessee, Old Hickory Lake a suburb of
Nashville and now resides in Rocklin, California near the bottom
basin of Tahoe National Forest, and Capitol City of Sacramento.

During a Traveling Excursion as a Nature
Photographer she produced images of Landscape
Scenes and Poetry to accompany "Winter Season with Nature"
throughout parts of the State in Idaho.

She has Traveled extensively in the United States and filmed in
remote locations on expeditions throughout the years including
the Big Island of Hawaii, Mexico, and British Columbia, Canada,
United Kingdom.

Forward

The State of Idaho is one of those best kept secret places for Travelers who have experienced coming to enjoy top Ski Resorts, outdoor Fishing and Boating in Lakes, and Rivers. Included is some of the best Hiking trails and Mountain Climbing in the Wilderness.

The area is known for Celebrities and retired people who come, and live here for the Season in Cabins or full-time. As well as many Military Veterans.

The Land is filled with River Rocks of Natural Earthtones.

In a wide Spectrum of localities throughout Idaho are spectacular Mountains, Hillsides and Farms passed on from many generations.

The area is comprised of Historical Barn structures throughout the Countryside. The vast Land is Prestine with Panoramic views. Country Houses, Cottages and Cabins out on Farms, in Forest, and rural settings paint a pretty picture of the beauty.

The land is Fertile with excellent Soil for growing Vegetables and Grape Vineyards. There are many Wineries throughout parts of Idaho.

The Native American Indian Tribes and Pioneers left behind Historical significance to Idaho. This includes people who came in Wagons to reach Idaho heading out on the Oregon Trail.

In the Capitol City of Boise, Idaho are many Basque people. The surrounding Farming communities once thrived on Wool produced from the Sheep Farms in vast regions at one time.

There is Fine Basque Restaurants in the downtown area serving daily meals of original Old World Cultural dishes going back to Traditions in Basque Country.

The Dairy Farms and Manufacturing buildings in the State of Idaho have top leading Milk, Butter, and Ice Cream products on the Market today found in Stores throughout the United States.

The Photography images in this book were filmed in parts of Boise, Idaho and rural towns. The places include Middleton, Caldwell, Meridian, Nampa, Emmett, and Twin-Falls known for the Snake River, and McCall, Idaho recognized as one of the top leading Tourist places to visit.

Aerial View of Idaho

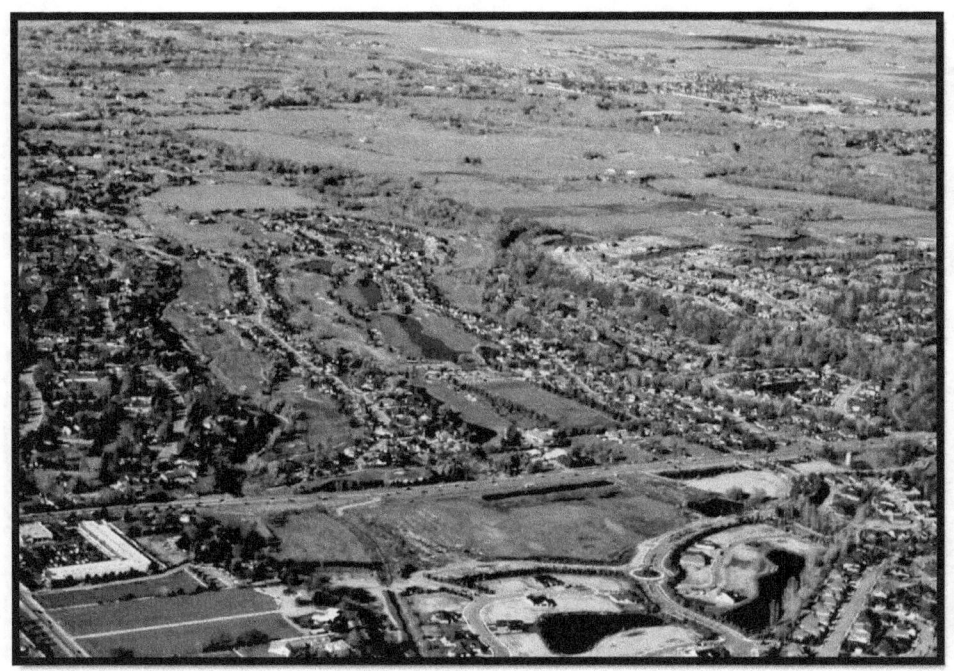

Mountains

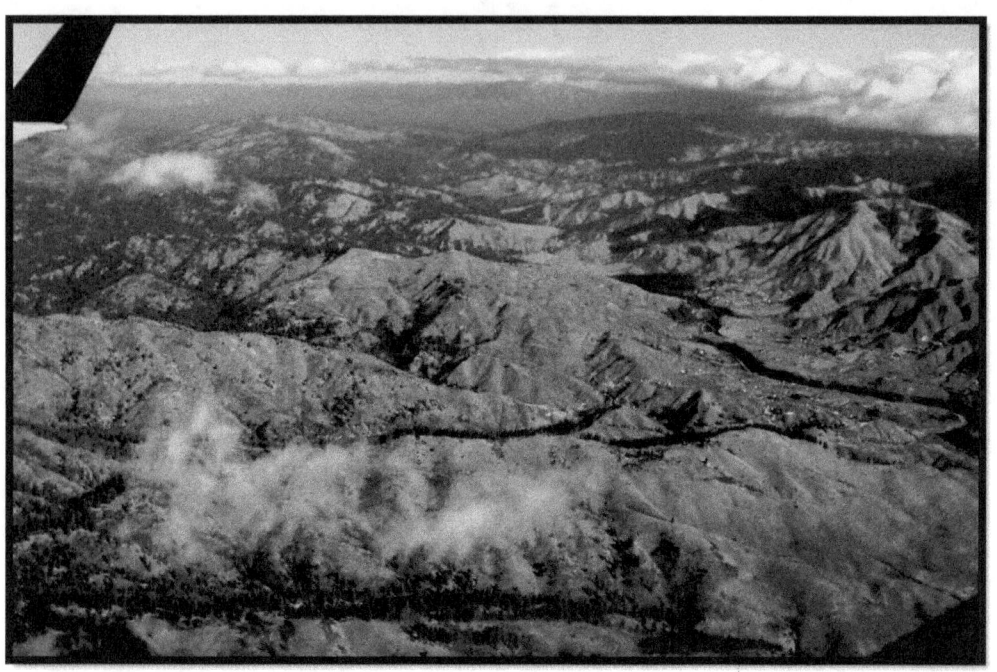

Hidden Estates, Valleys and Farms

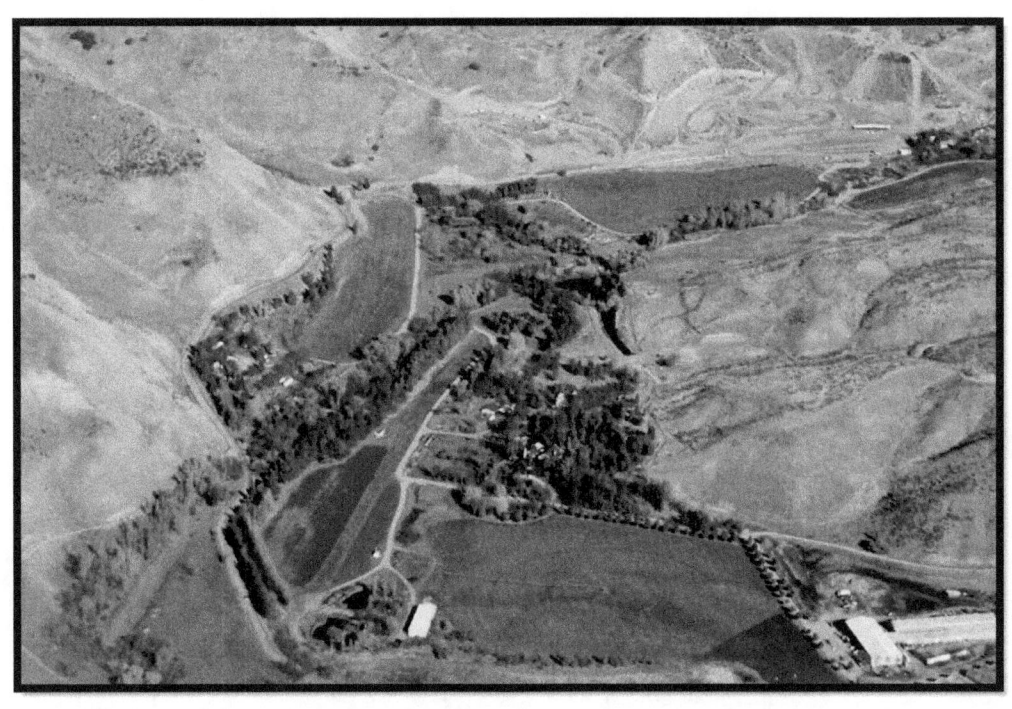

Vast Rivers and Lakes

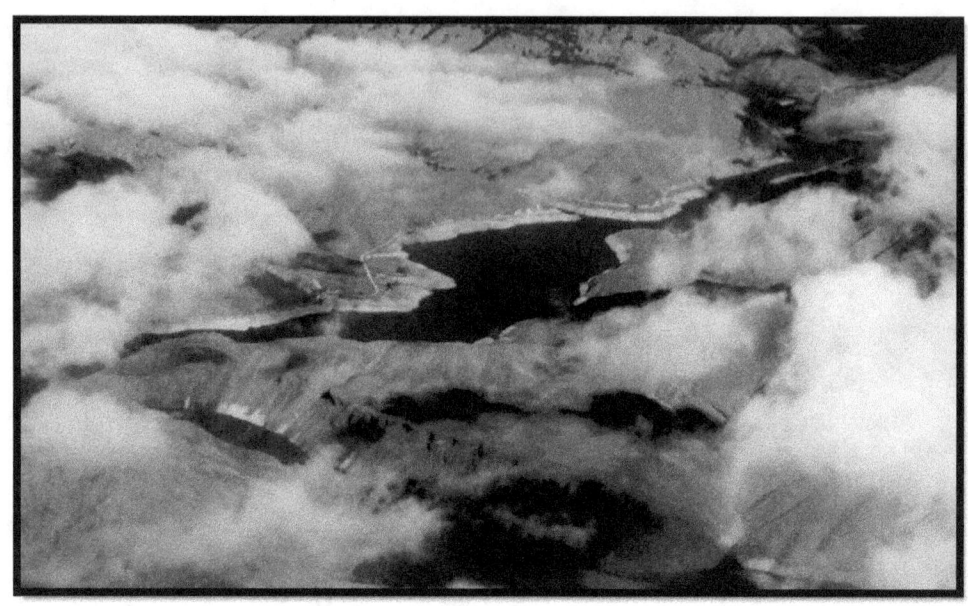

State Capitol of Boise, Idaho

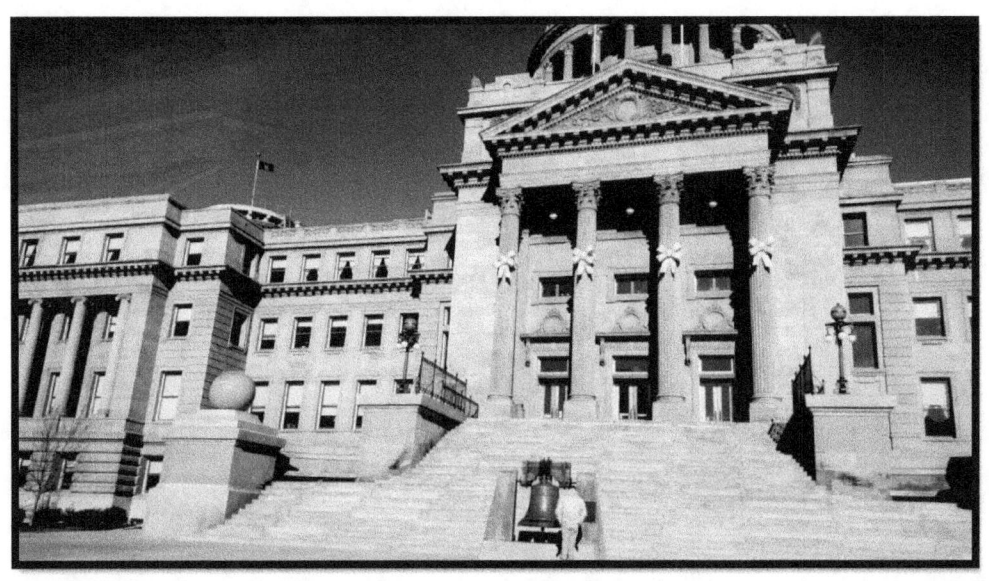

White Hooting Owls

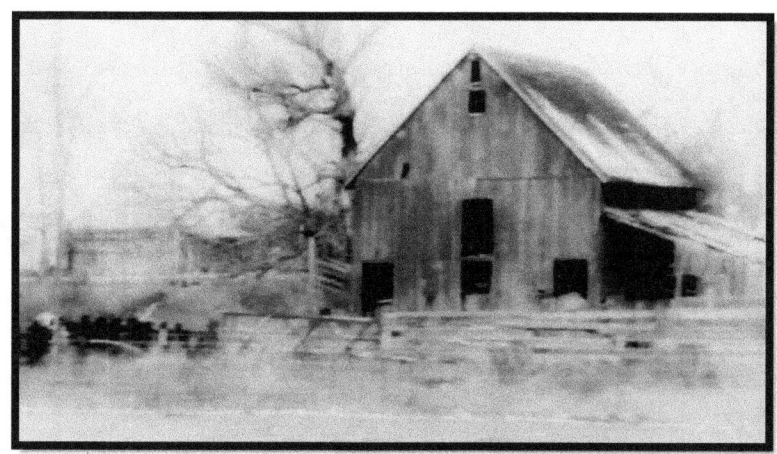

Perched on top of the inside Barn is a flock of Snow

Owls taking positions of dominance.

They are Hooting away early morning.

As a women wearing a cream colored Cotton dress

Walks to her Mailbox. The Country Dogs follow

her down the Road as Cars go on by honking

a friendly hello.

Starkness

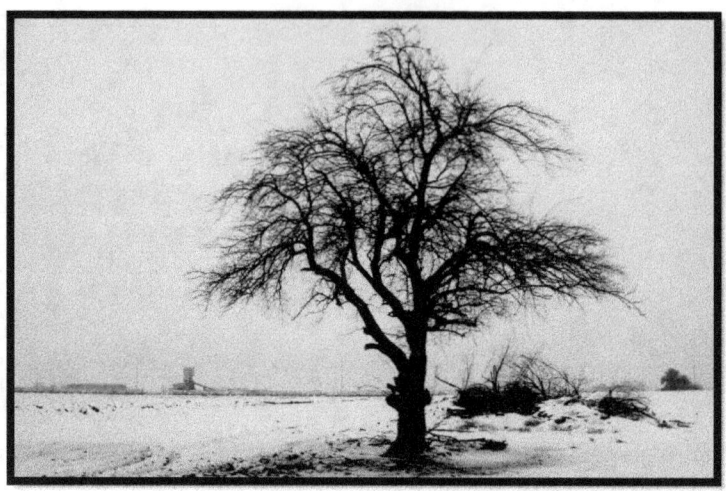

Left alone during a Winters Snow storm

A Tree stands in Starkness of a dreary day.

Dairy Farms are seen in a distance

as the Fog hangs around with bitter

coldness as another storm heads its way.

Misty Fog

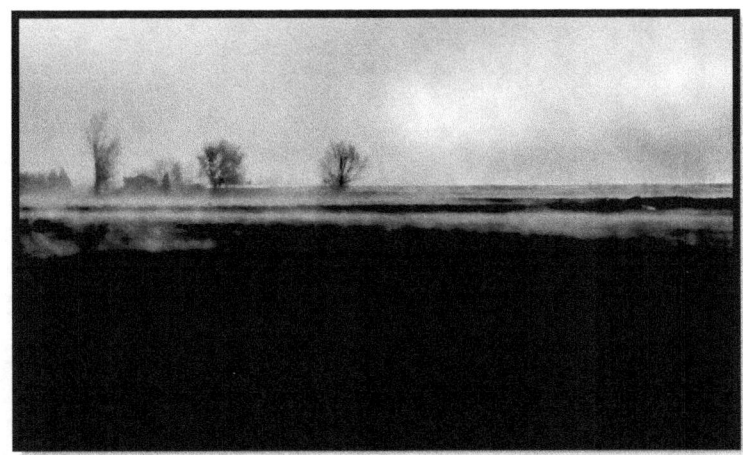

Creeping along the open fields near the highway

Misty Fog makes it's way across the Land.

The Sun tries to shine through the thick Fog.

Oak Trees are in stillness.

The Valley people are sound asleep.

Winter Leaves

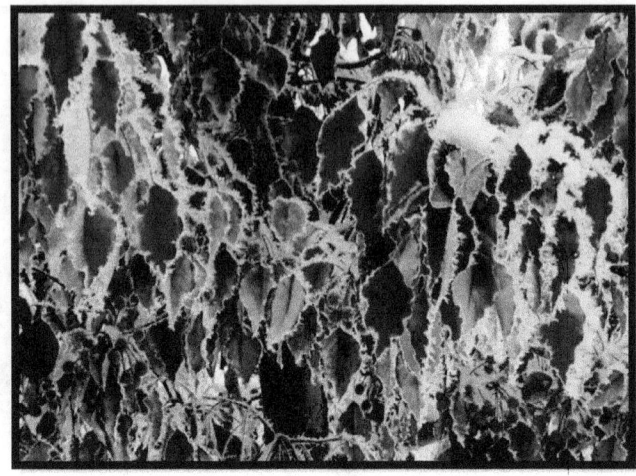

Hundreds of Fruit leaves in colors of Orange

and Yellow with Brown are Frozen.

They leave a trace that Winter is still upon the Land.

When Spring arrives the coldness will be gone and

the Peach Blossoms will come again.

Basque Two-Story House

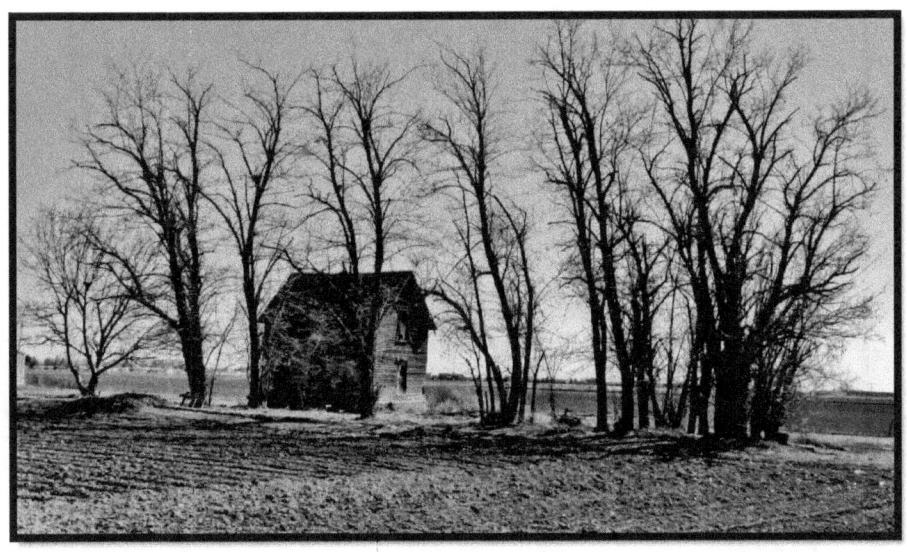

Off the Beaten path is a Basque two-story house

Sitting alone in the distance from the rest of the world.

Dirt Roads lead to far away places

and Tall trees stretch up to the sky.

Boulders in the Forest

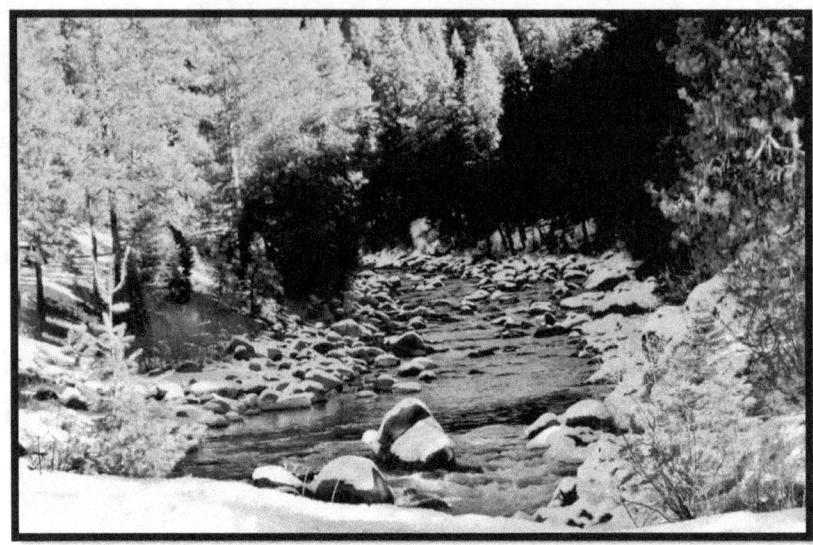

Black and Grey boulders are covered with Snow.

Driving through the Boise Forest on windy roads

with views of Mountain tops and rushing Rivers.

As travelers speed along roads on a Sunny day

making their way to Ski resorts and Cabins in the

woods of McCall, Idaho.

Shadows

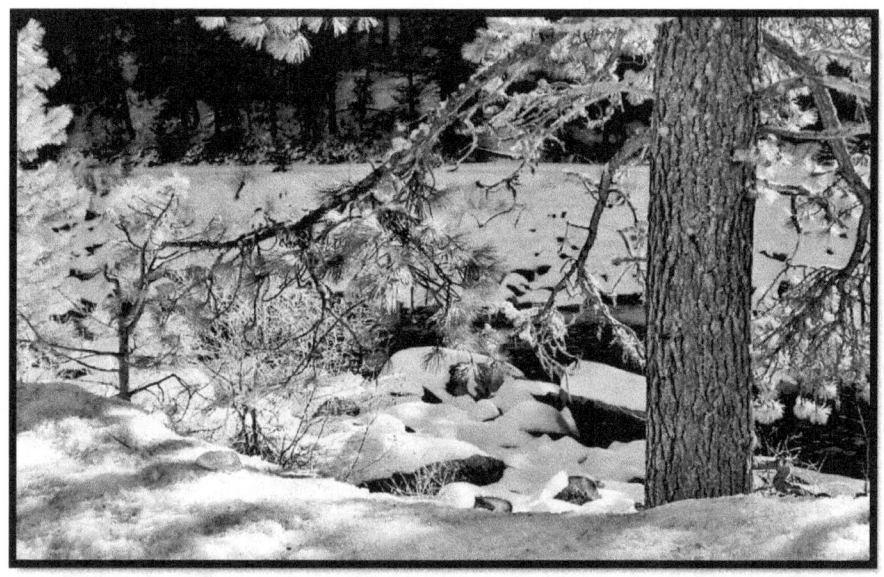

Afternoon Shadows fill the Boise Forest of

movement like a time-clock just ticking away.

Thoughts of Simplicity fill ones mind

while watching Cross-Country Skiers

go on by into the Wilderness.

Land and Sky

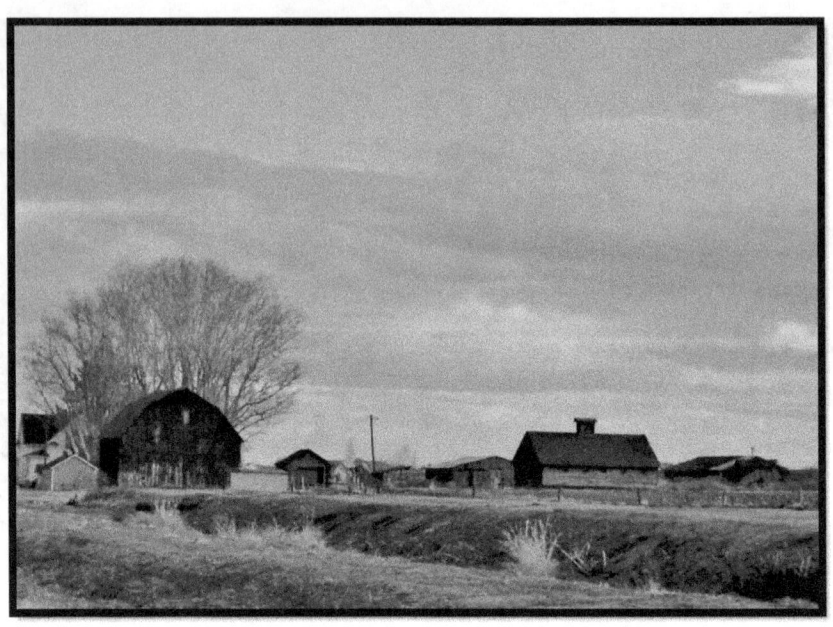

Cloudes across the Sky

Amish Barn

Tool Crib

Horse Barn

Trees

Colonial home off to the side.

Boise Snowscape

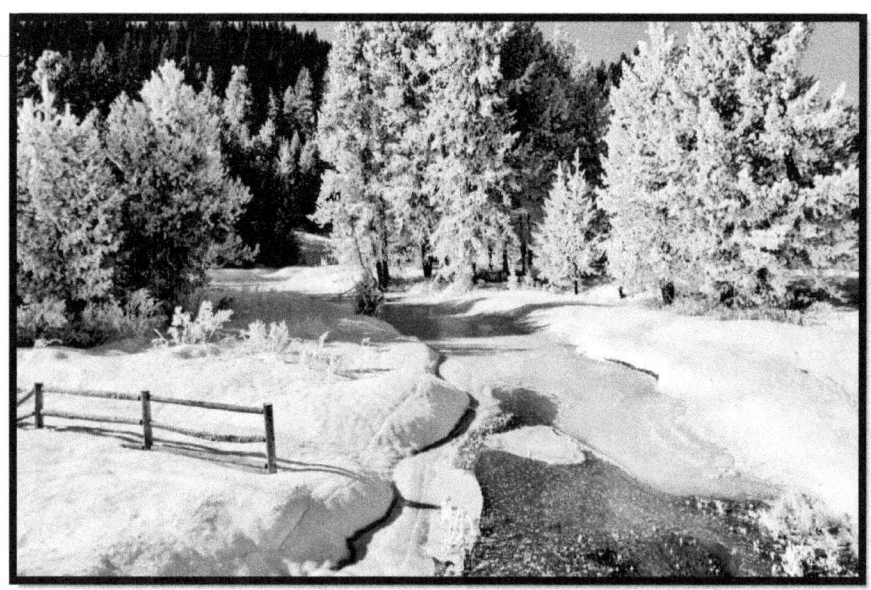

Frozen River on the outskirts

of the the Boise National Forest

leads to a Path onto a Trail in the Woods.

A Wooden Fence and Snow like Frosting

surrounded by the

Morning Sunlight was drenched in Beauty.

Farmhouse and Path

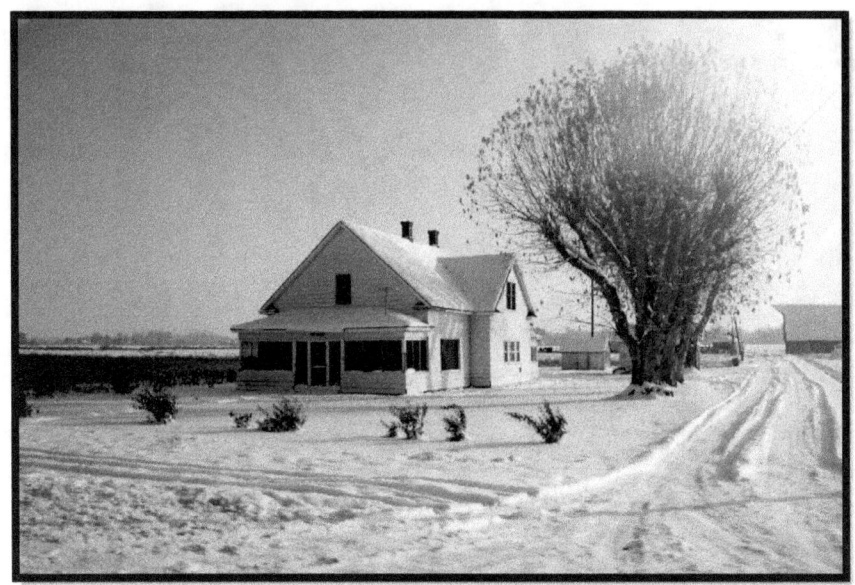

A Country Home in Middleton

with a Snow Path leading to a Barn.

A Cattle Farm with Trees and the Sun out.

Milk Bottles out on an Old Porch with

Laundry hanging inside to dry.

American Quarter Horse

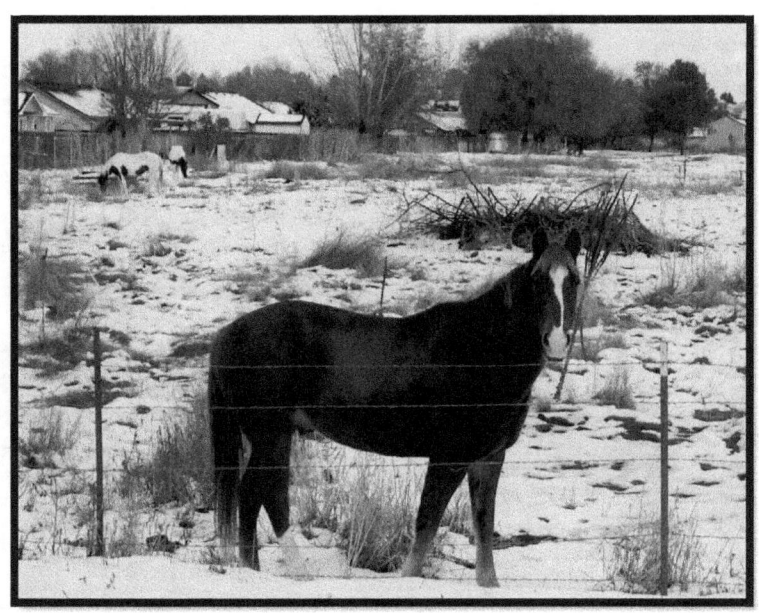

Snow covered field

A Horse of Beauty

Stillness

during early morning out for a walk.

The Village

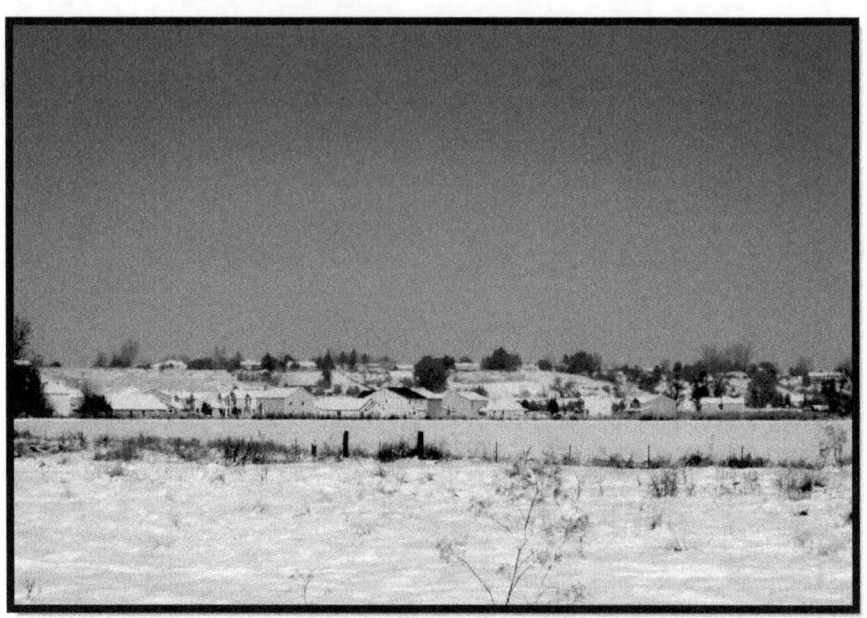

Sun came out

The Village people are still Sleeping.

Footprints in the Snow

Long awaken day.

Tall Oak Trees

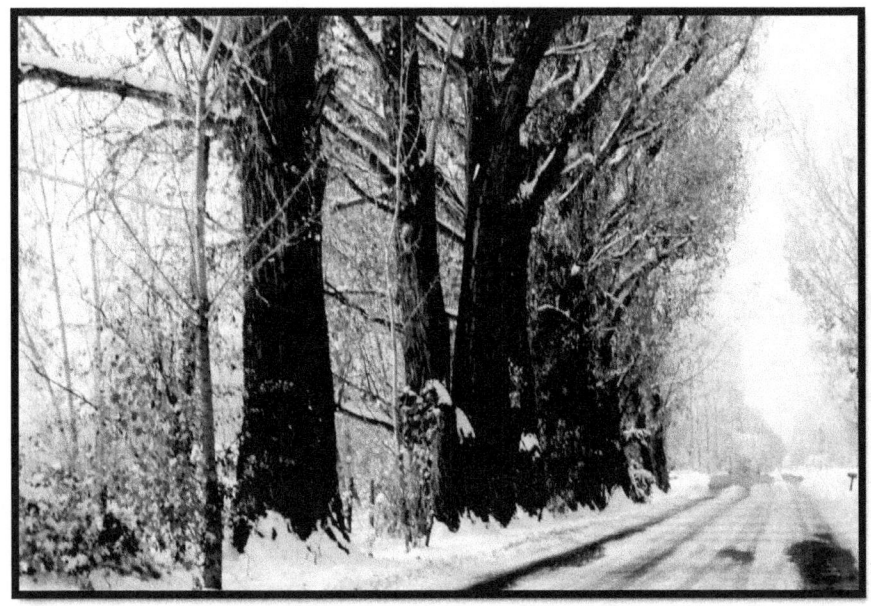

Timber trees

Tall and Strong

Black Ice on Road

Heading to the Post Office

on a cold Winters day.

Old School House

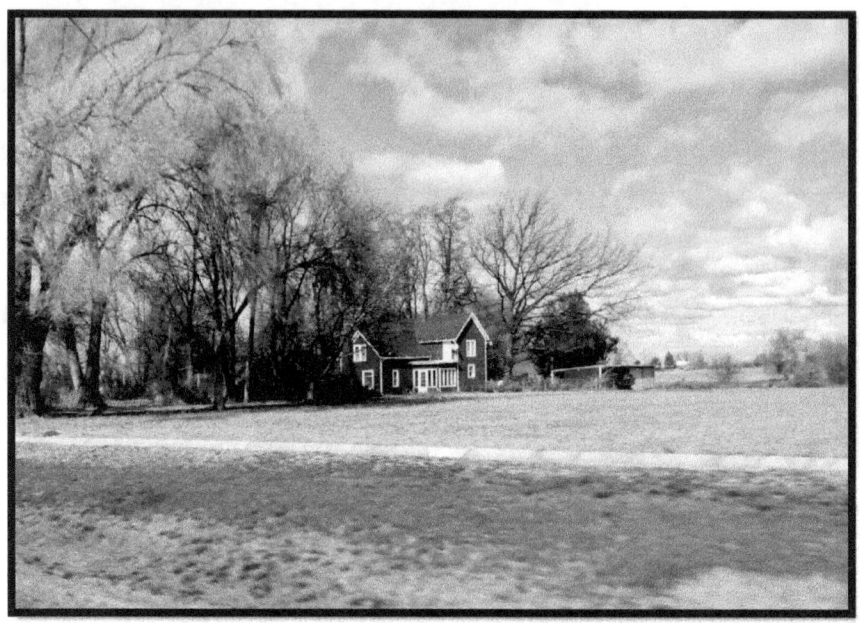

Country home like an Old School House.

It has a Front Porch and is Two-Stories.

In the distance is surrounding tall Trees.

A Black Labrador comes running down the Road

to meet his loved ones.

Frozen Maple Leaves

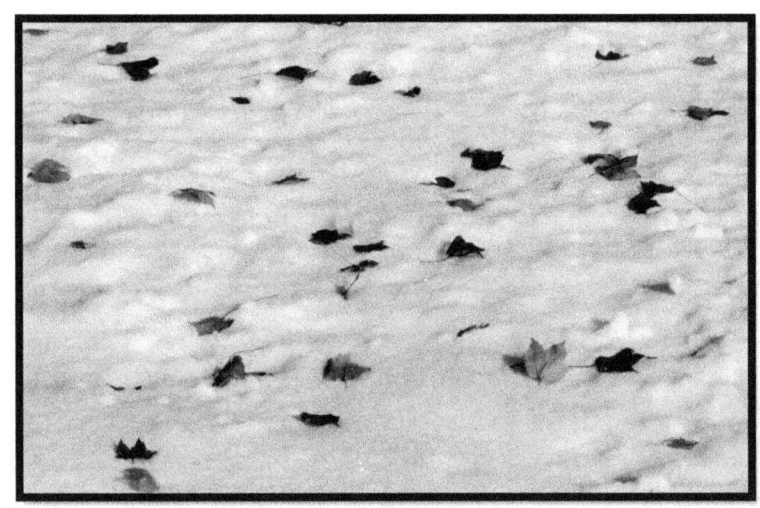

Snow among the Maple Leaves

Frozen in Time.

Snowman

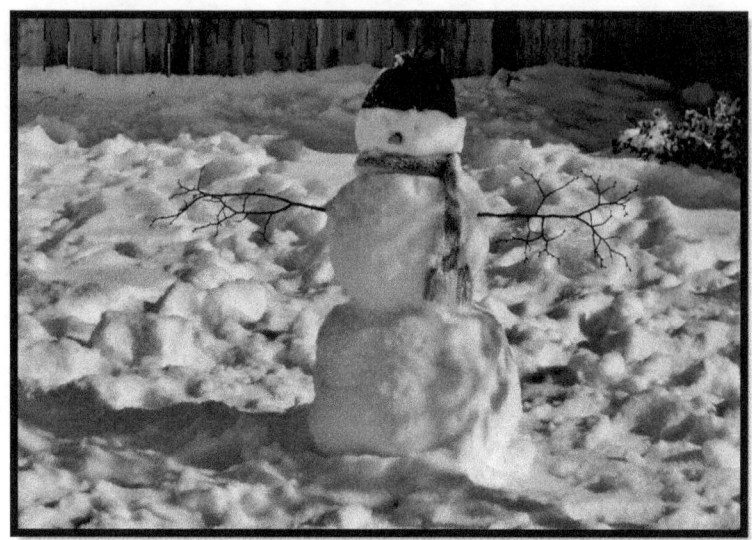

Winter Season

During Christmas

The laughter of Children in the Village

Go out to play

and build Snowman all day.

Tires and Farm Barn

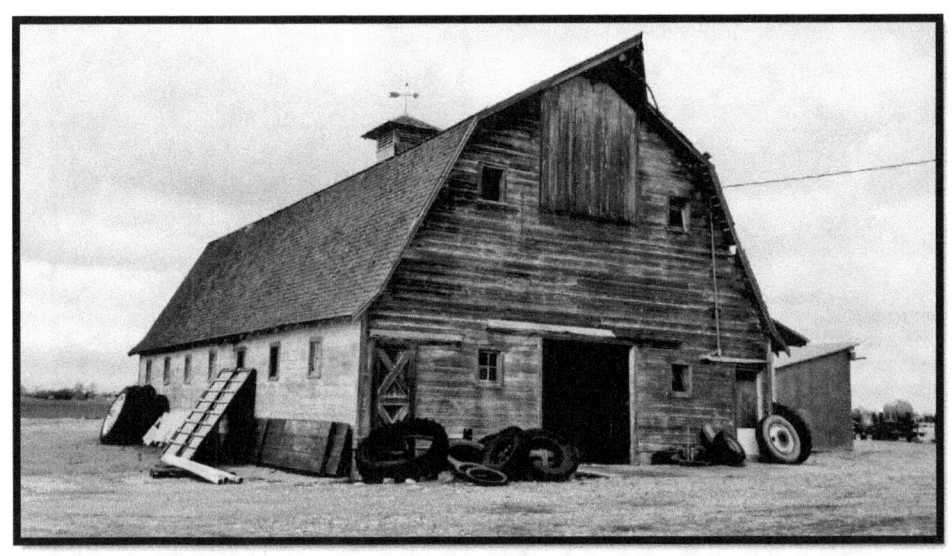

Tractor Tires surround the Barn.

The Farming workers go home early

as Cloudes roll on in and the

Rain keeps on coming down.

Dawn of the Day

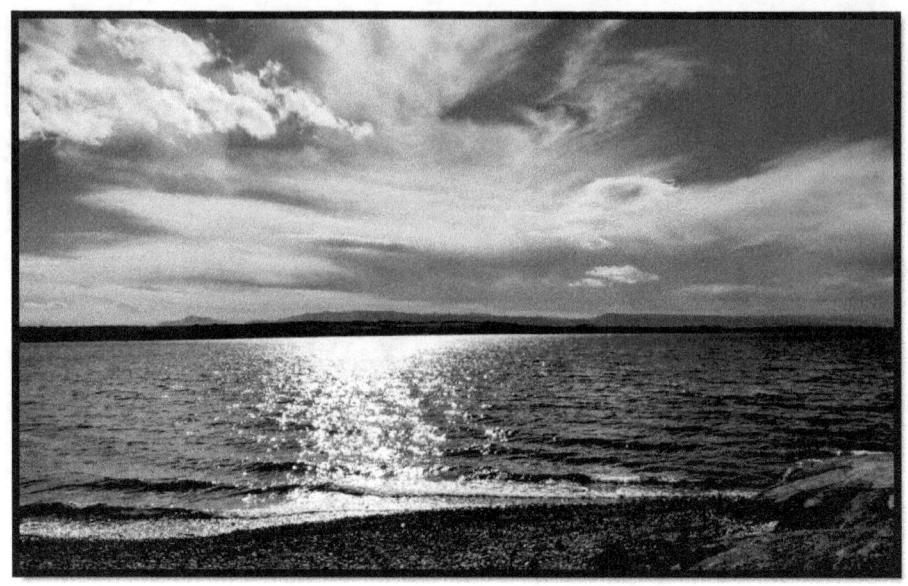

Pelicans and Ducks swimming in the Lake

as Tides roll in and out on the Shore.

Sunset before dusk

Stillness surrounds the Woods

as one throws Pebbles into the Water

and walks away.

Sculptor Driftwood

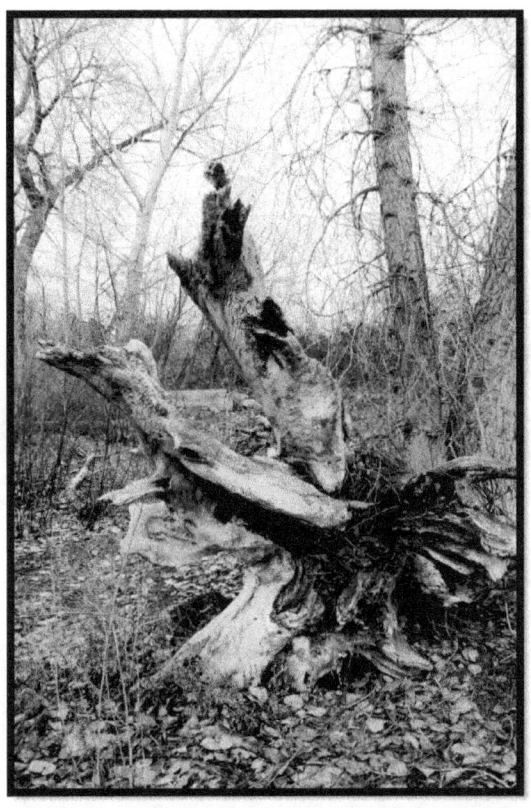

Like a Sculptor of large Wings

Driftwood harbors in Beauty

as that of Form and Style making

Movement like a dancer.

Two Leaves

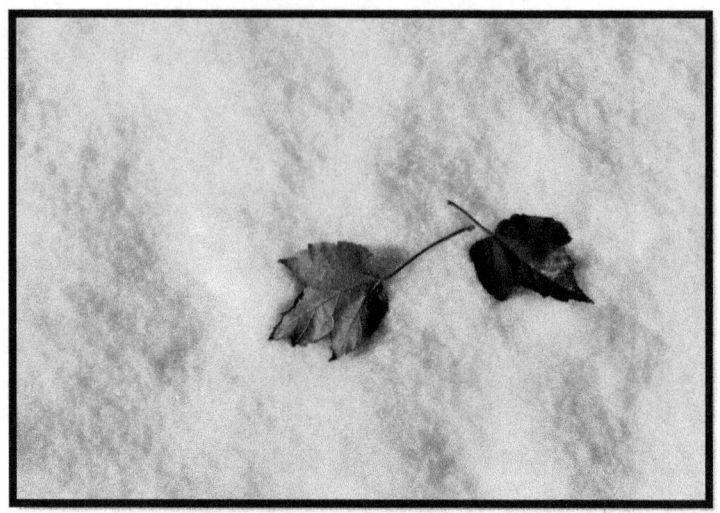

Leaves fallen in the Snow

Warmth of the Sun

Color of Red as Love

Binds them as they Cling to their existance

holding steady.

Ghost of the Past

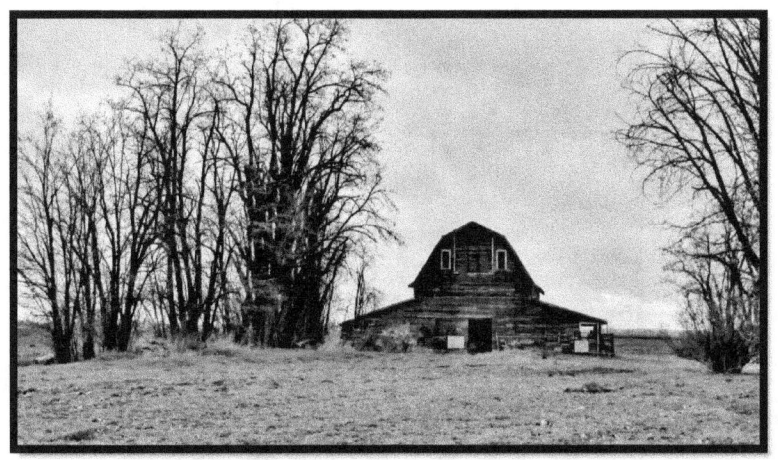

There it was a Barn sitting alone and it was

as if it was staring right at your face.

Near the front door entrance

was the figure of a Man from long ago

as quickly as he came he vanished right before

ones own very eyes.

It was as if it was never there to begin with

though in Spirit he was still around.

Tree Branches

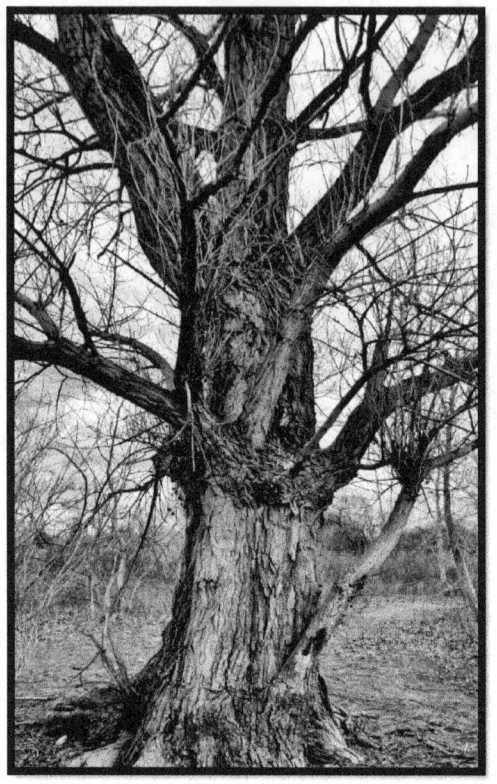

Branches Outstretched

Nature and Beauty

Horses Grazing

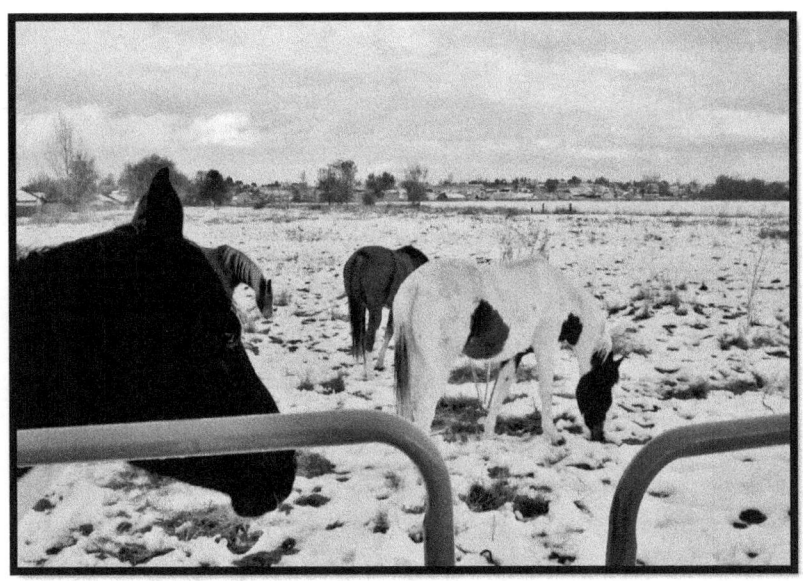

Horses grazing Hay in an open field. The

American Quarter Horses, Pinto and Appaloosa

come to greet one at the gate.

Cloudes come a Rolling in

calling out for Rain tonight.

Flowing River

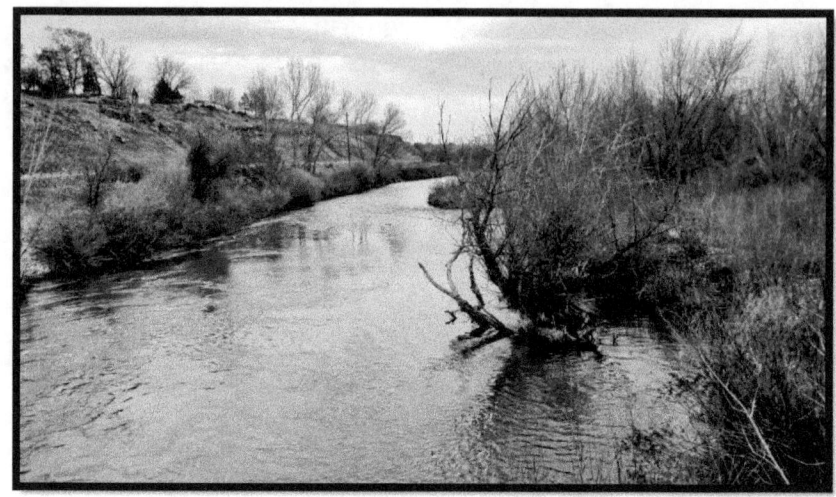

The Boise River flows so free

even in late Winter Season when all

the Tree Branches are stark with

no leaves. Up on the Hillside one can hear

an Old Hound Dog howling as a Raccoon takes

off running to play hide and seek in the

nearby meadow.

Stream and Fence

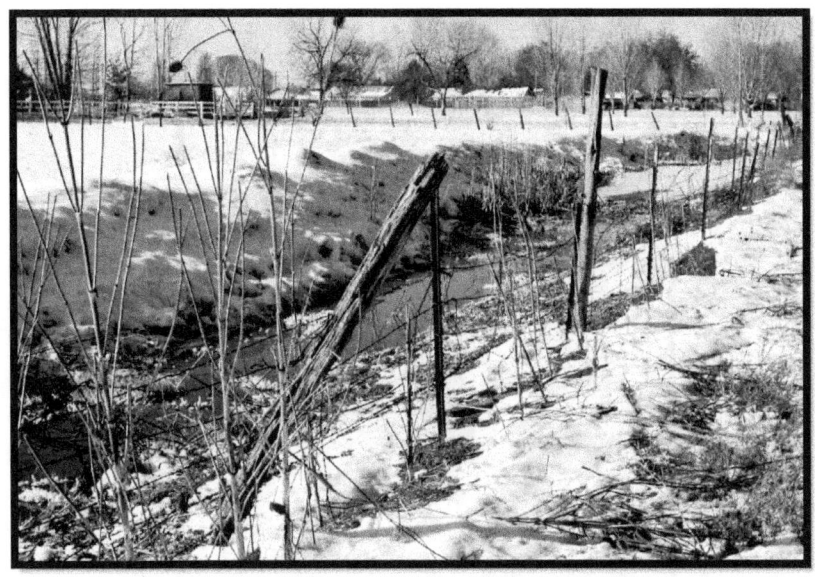

Wooden Fence and Boise River

Early morning Stillness

Walking and collecting

Pebble Rocks

with the Sunlight Shining so bright

and Rabbits go Running to hide.

Morning Snow

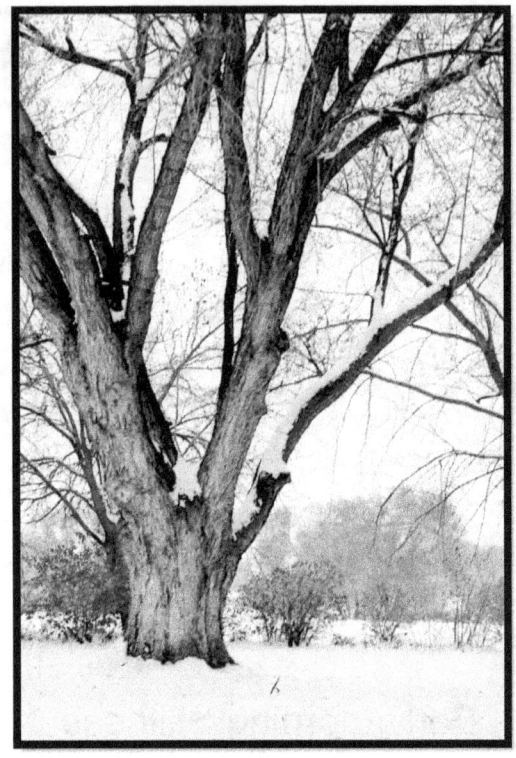

She sat out underneath the Trees in

Summertime Reading and Writing books of

Poetry with her Cats, and Dogs.

It is now Wintertime and she is much older

now remembering good times of youth.

The Dairy Farm

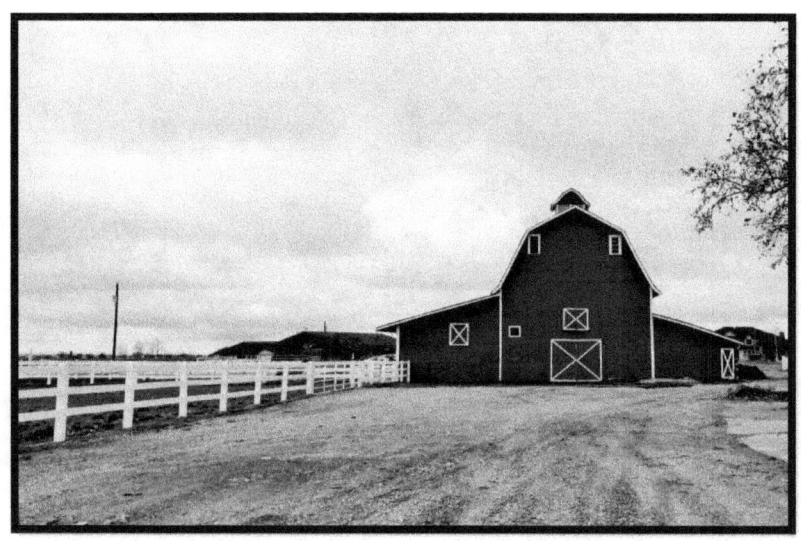

The Dairy Farm Barn sits tucked away in

Red and White color tones along a Fenceline.

A place for Roosters, Cows and Horses to stay

all year round.

Place in the Mountains

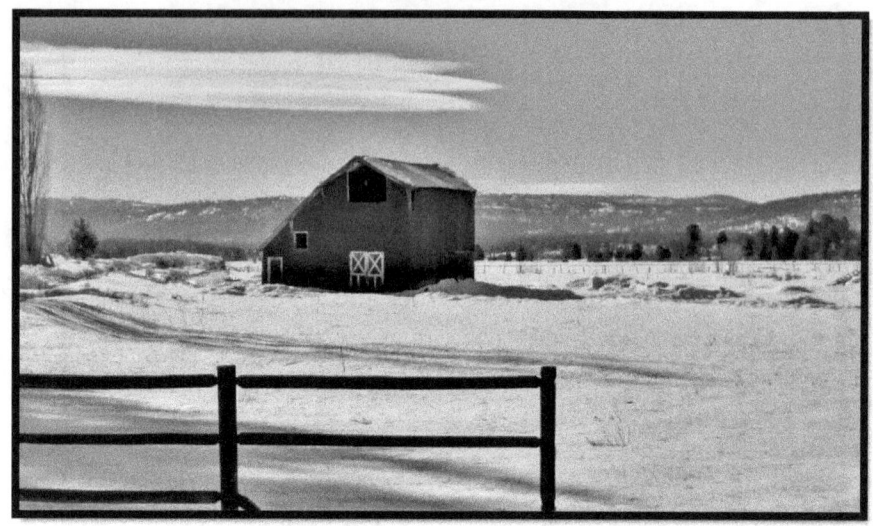

Fences and Snow

Light Shadows

Cow Barn

Cabins and Hillsides in the distance.

Country Farm Ranchers

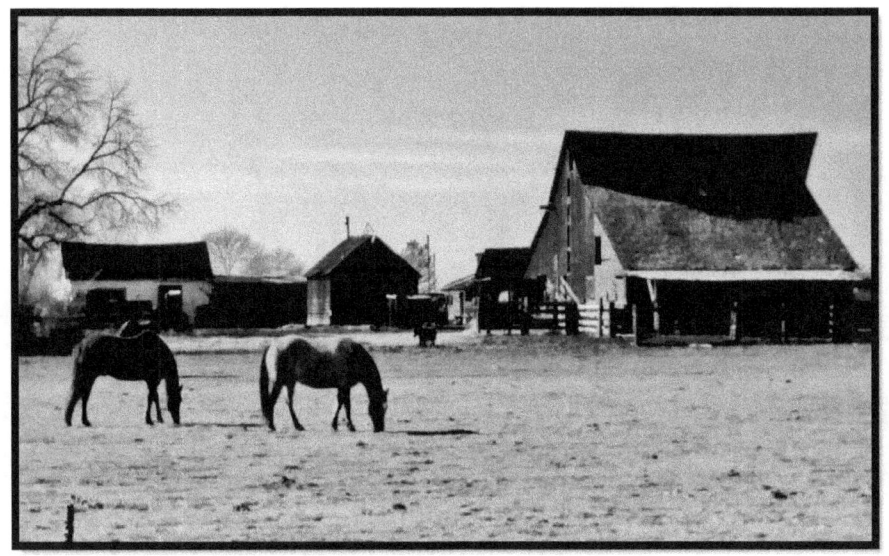

Horses grazing on the Grass

Country White House

Barrels of Water for the Animals to drink

on a Sunday lazy day in March.

River Canyons

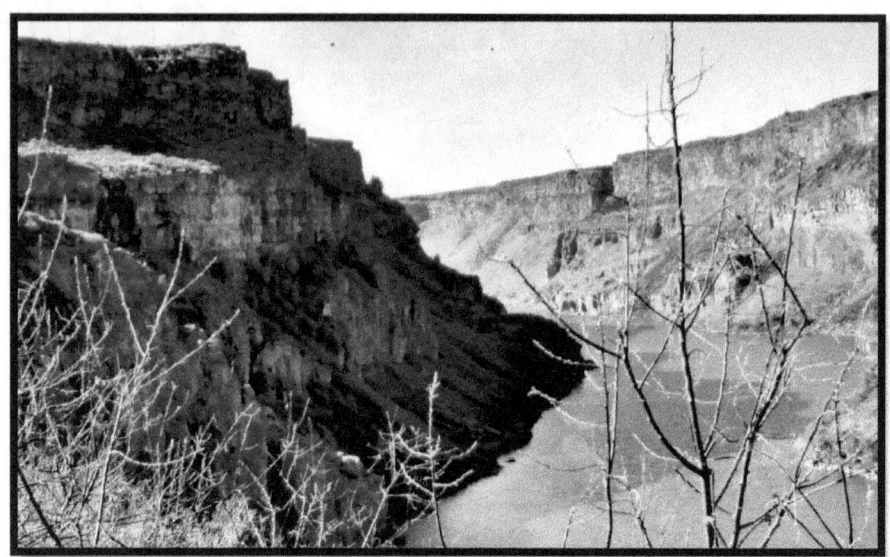

Steep terrain in the River Canyons

Sacred paths from long ago.

Indians once gathered here

and lived among the Water

in Peace on Native land.

Waterfalls

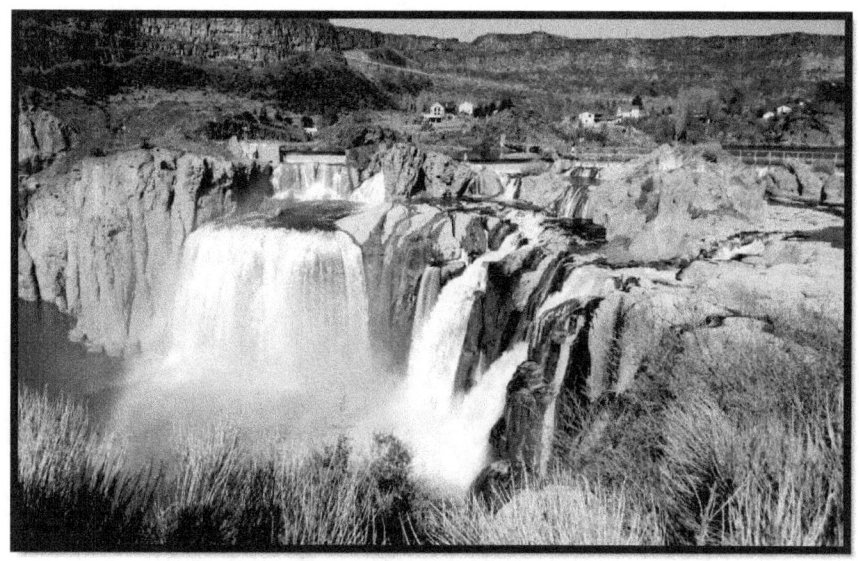

Sacred Water

Canyons

Village of Fisherman

Dove flying overhead

Double Rainbows

God our Creator is great.

Sacred Land

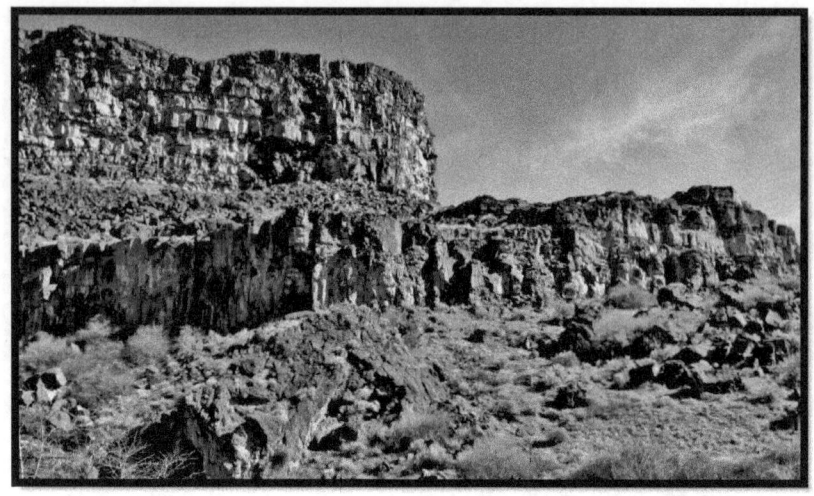

Deep Red and Burnt Umber Soil

The Sacred Land

of Canyons embrace

those from the past and the present

as One people.

Rock Carvings

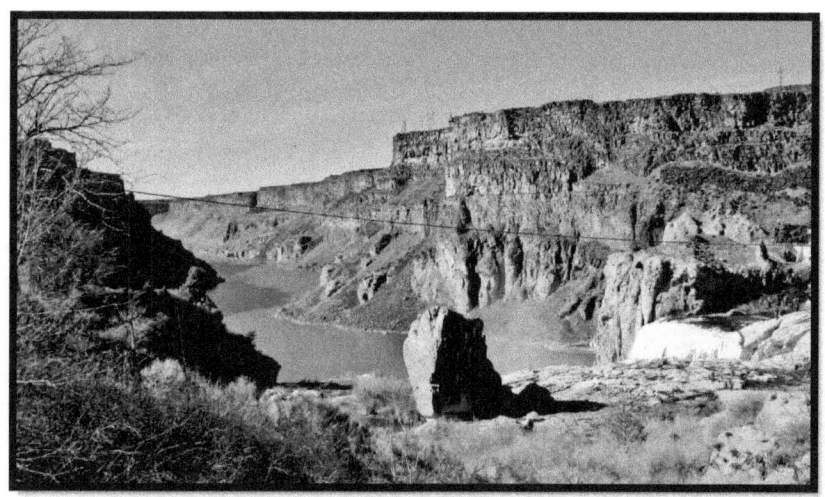

Etched upon the Rocks are

Signs from those who lived here long ago.

Signature markings in the Canyon and

near the River of Fish a Eagle

Soars across the Morning Sky.

Ancient Faces in the Caverns

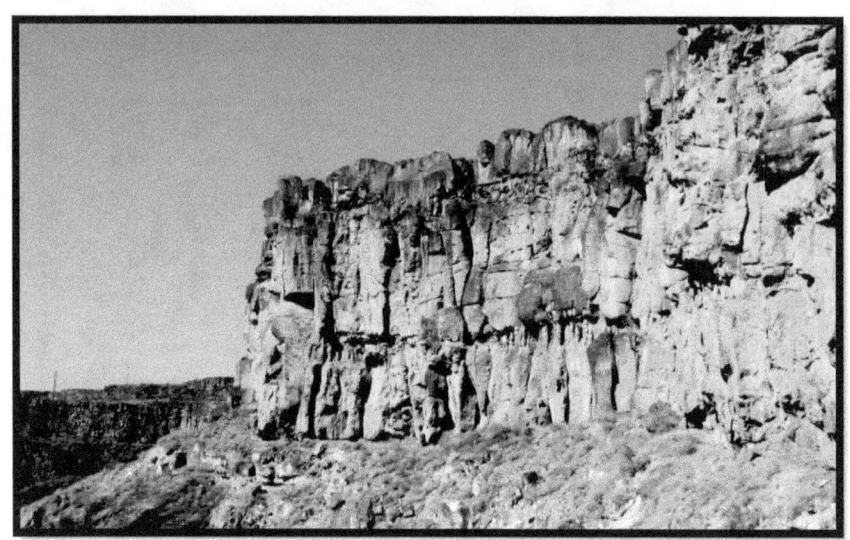

On the Face of Rocks in the Caverns

are of Warrior Men overlooking the Canyon.

They stand so proud and tall

as if Saluting their Chief.

Snake River

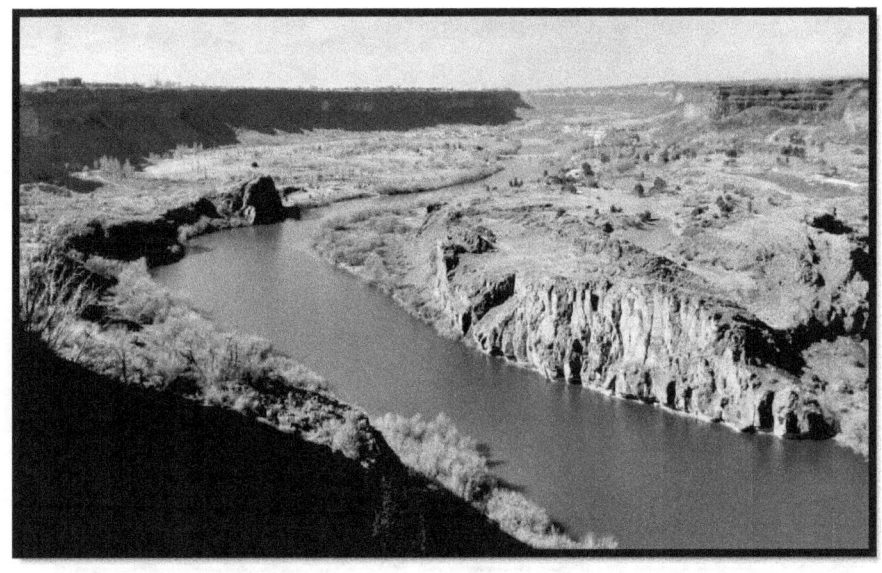

Long

Curvy

Snake River

Canoes

Indians

Fishing for food.

Barn Cats

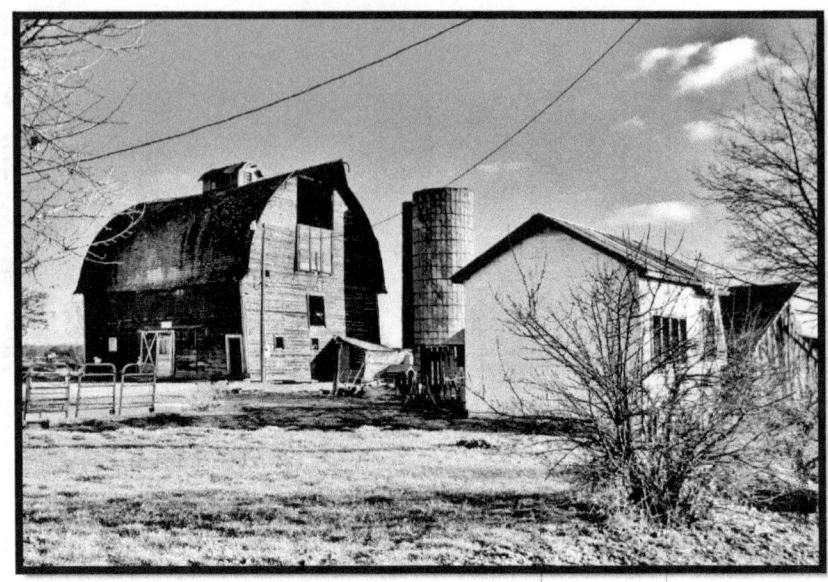

Country Milk

Barn Cats

Playing outside near the Shed

while the mother sits watching the

Young she protects their Habitat.

Pioneers and Horses

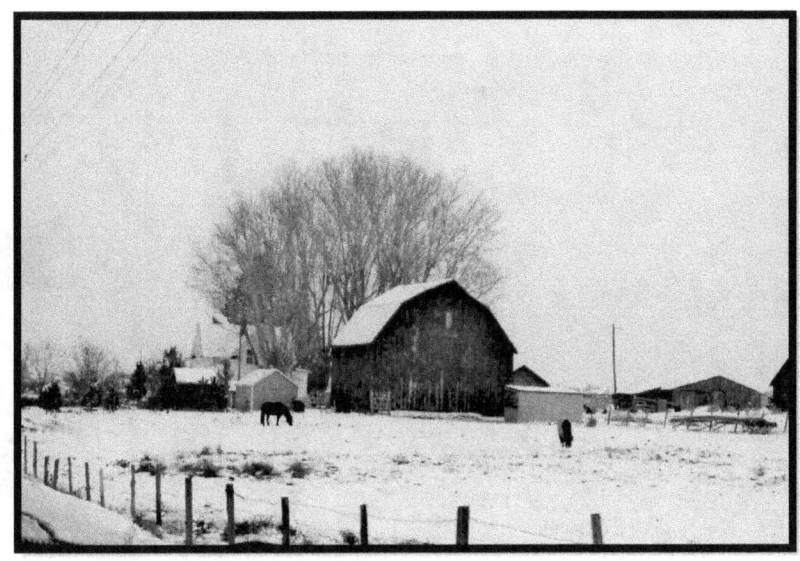

Horses and Carriages.

Homesteaders

Trails from long ago

Amish and Basque Farms

Valley of plenty.

Amish Barn on the Hillside

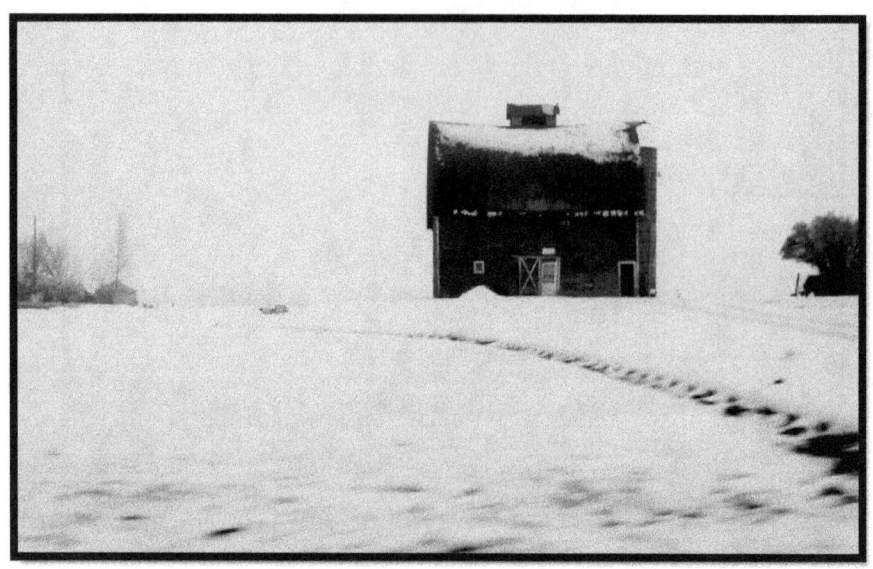

Wooden Wagon climbs up the Path

Snow covered Hillside

Amish Barn

Winter Coldness.

Butterfly Leaves

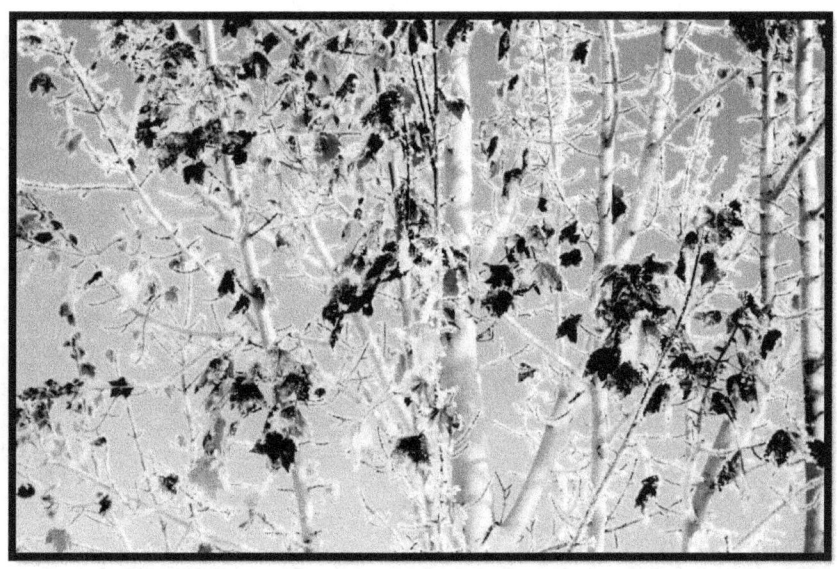

Leaves of today hanging on Trees

Crystal Glass as Ice

Stillness

Rising to the Morning

Blue Sky

Butterflies Captured

Waiting for the Sun to set them free.

Structures

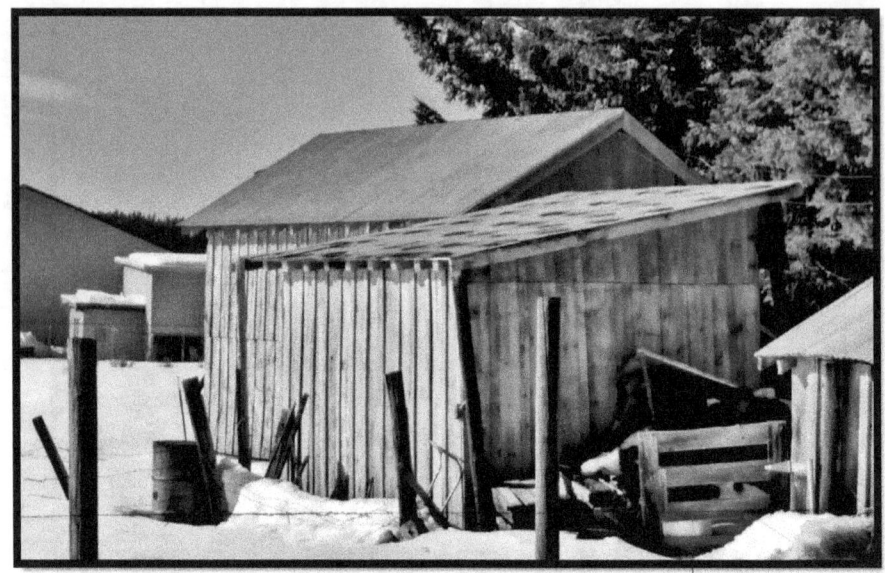

Line formations

Tall Wooden Poles

Crate Barrels

Sheds

A Settlers Homestead.

Pine Tree

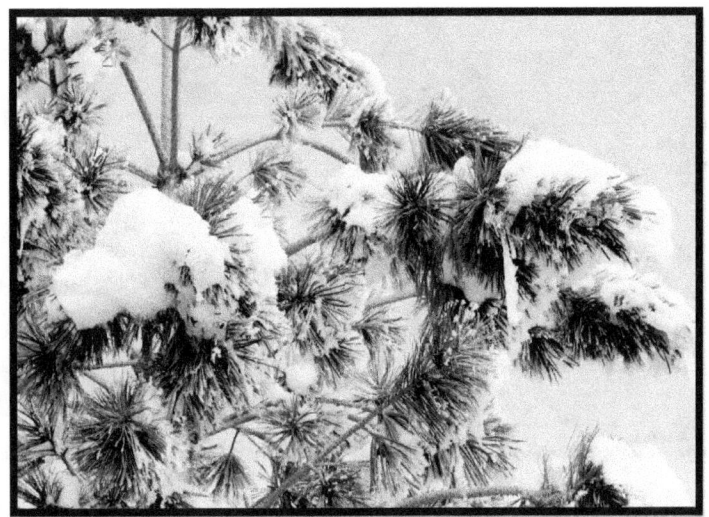

Morning Brisk Air

Country General Store nearby

Pine Tree covered in Snow

A Man walks up in his Blue Jacket

while Smoking a Cigar. He is

wearing Gloves and a Muffled Hat

to cover his ears.

Vacant House

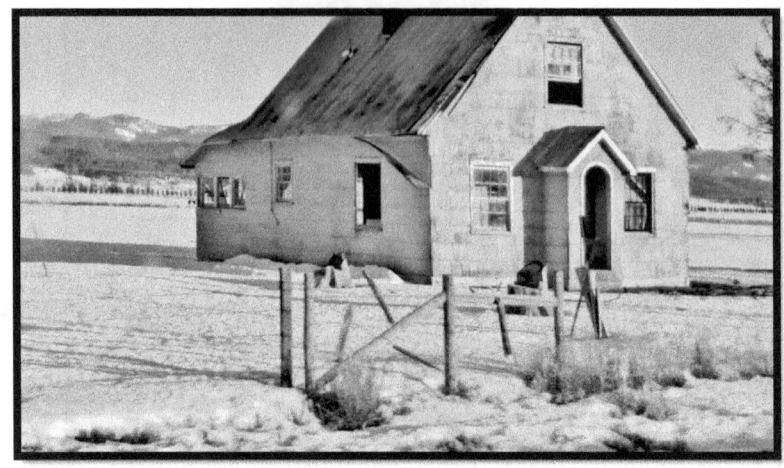

Archway

Door

Broken Window Pane

Vacant House in the Valley

from drifters who have moved away.

Winter Trees

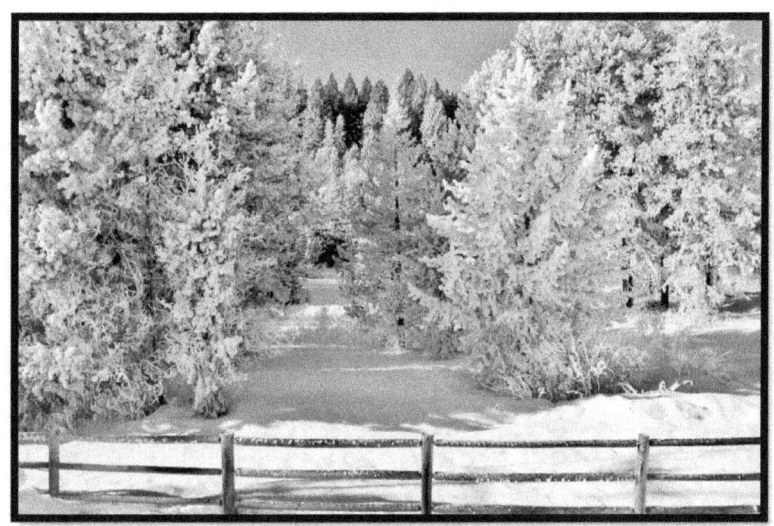

Snow

Frosted Trees

Fence

Morning

Sun

Valley

Beauty.

Open Road

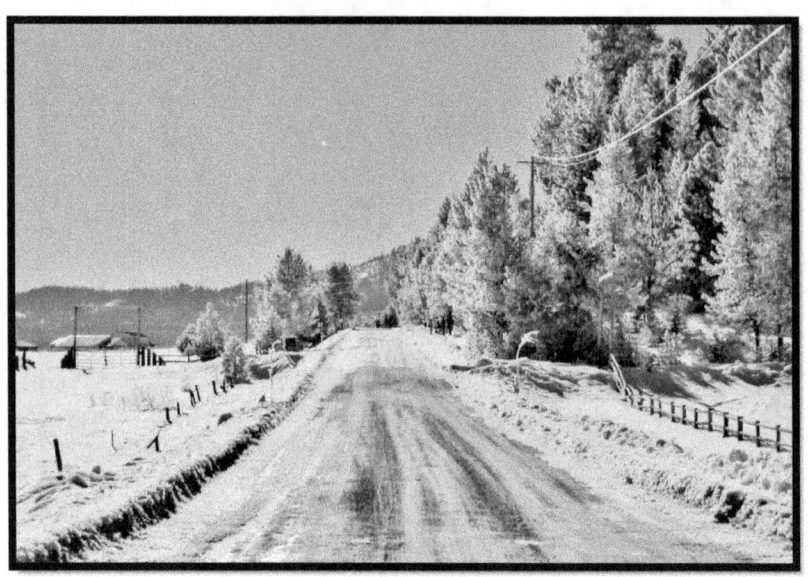

Sun and Moon

White Snow looked like Vanilla Icing

covered upon the Countryside land

of places only travelers dreamed of coming

up to in their Cars.

These paths lead to beautiful homesteads

filled with Horses and Riding arenas for Cowboys.

High Country

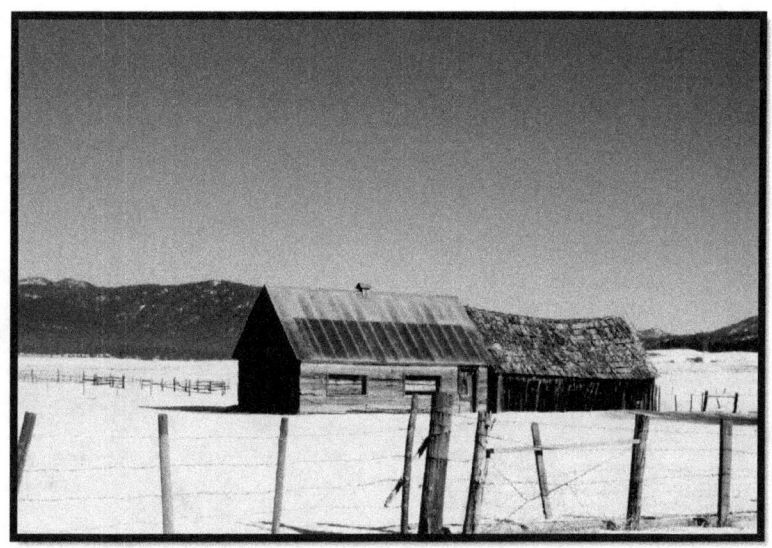

Wooden Fences outstretched for miles.

Closed up Windows in Barns

keep the fierce Winter Wind from blowing inside.

Open Space

Beauty

Cascades

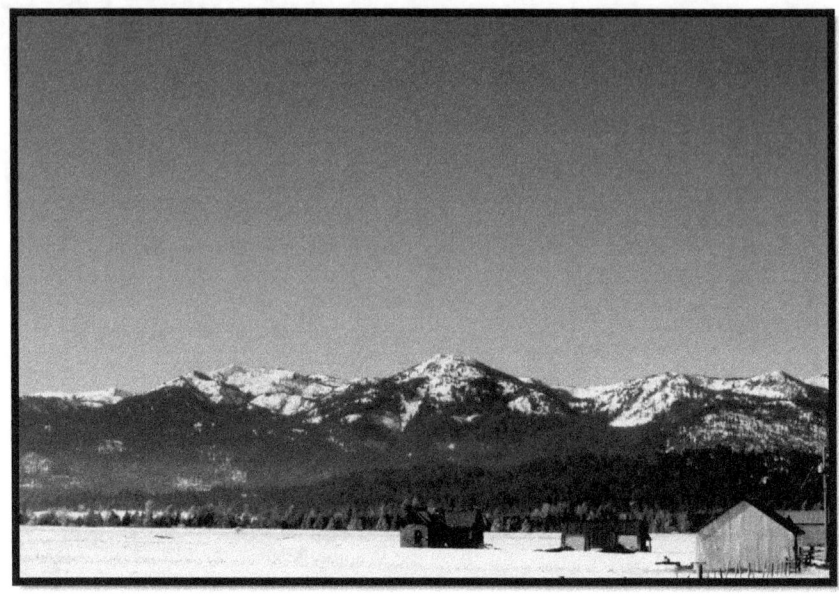

The Cascade Mountain Peaks in the distance

Cabins

Abandoned

Red Fox and Timerline Wolf running freely

Open Terrain.

Sun and Shed

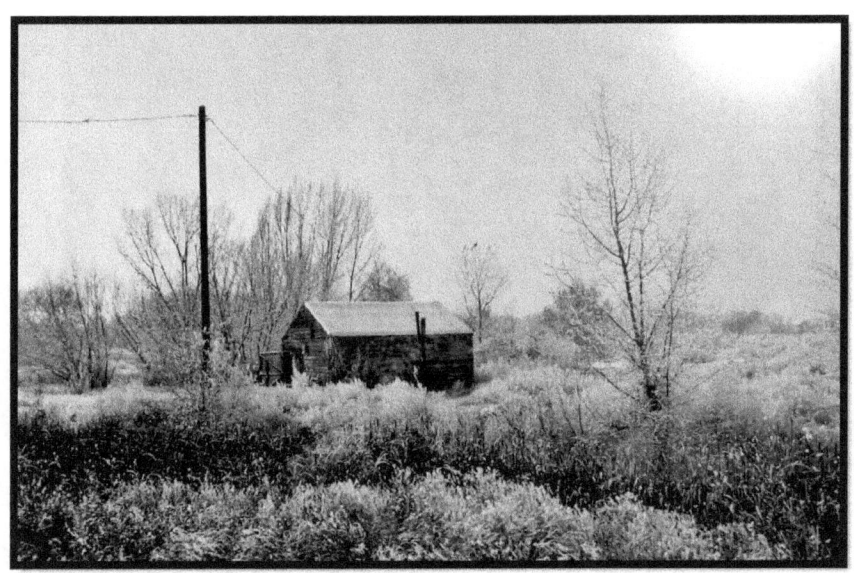

Settlers Shed

Sunshine

Frozen Branches on Trees

Squirrels play up in the Trees

Sound of Water

Flowing downstream.

Hidden in the Woods

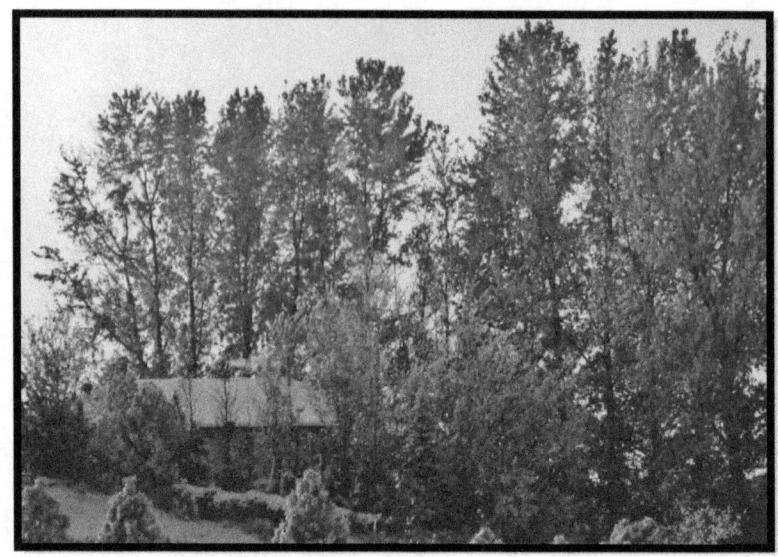

Wooden Cabin hidden in the Woods

Nestled among Forest trees.

Stone fence lines up the Path

Smoke from the Fireplace is seen

Timber Logs stacked in piles outdoors

while inside a Cup of Hot Coffee is being brewed.

Beauty of Stillness

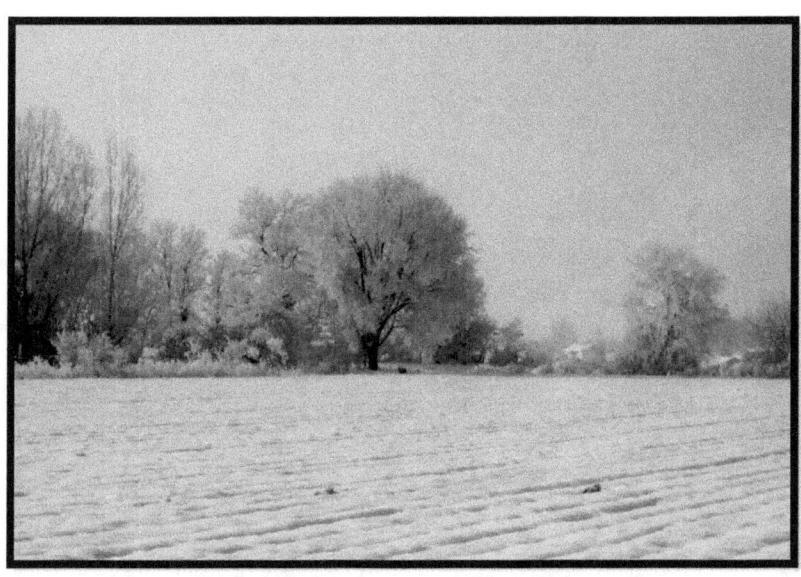

Standing in the forefront of others in the Center

is a Tree of Beauty surrounded by the Winter Snow

which has fallen.

Open fields lay lined up waiting for the Sun.

Workers Truck

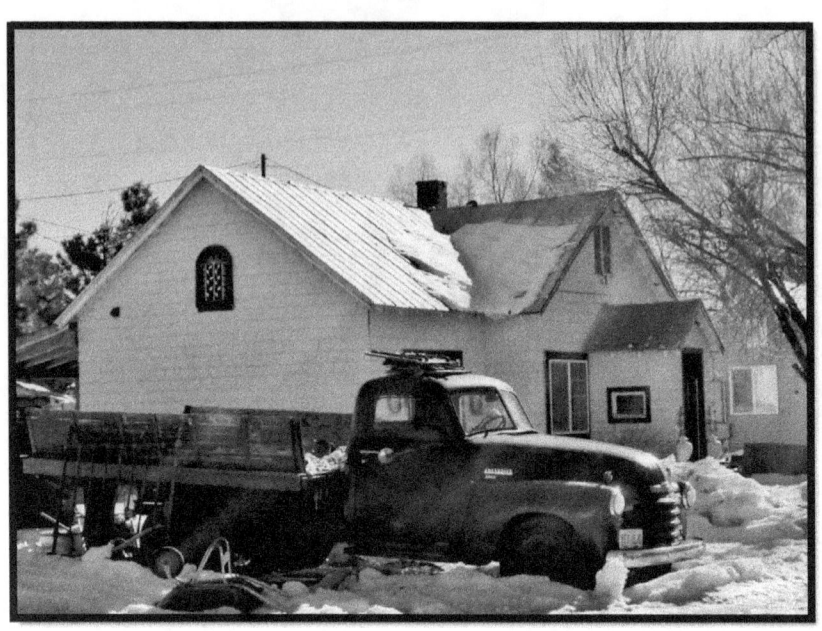

Country Cottage and Sleepy Village

Homemade Breads in the Oven

Classic Truck

Man Waving

Good morning.

Cottages

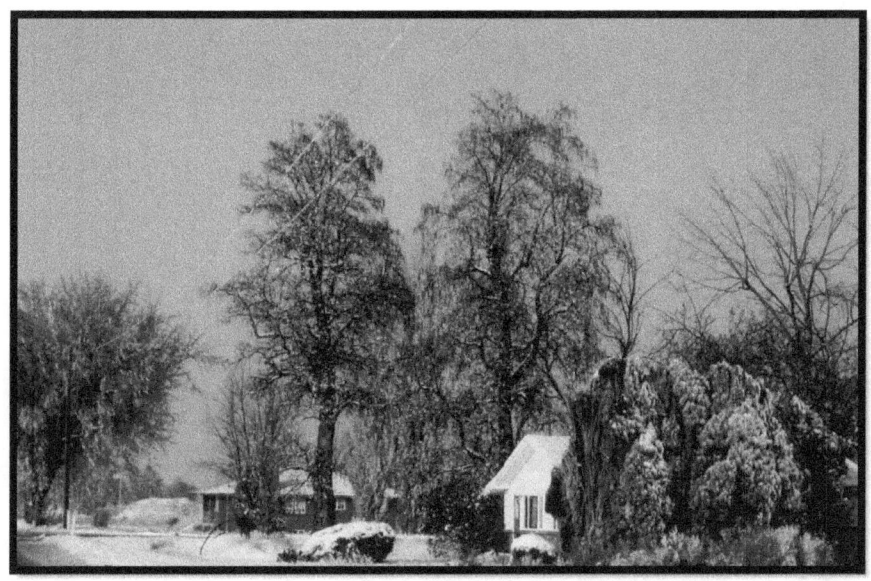

Places where the elderly live and retire

from days in the beaten Sun

of working on Farmlands of yesterday.

They nestle among the Trees in a safe Haven

so close to their Heart where they now stay.

Path in Life

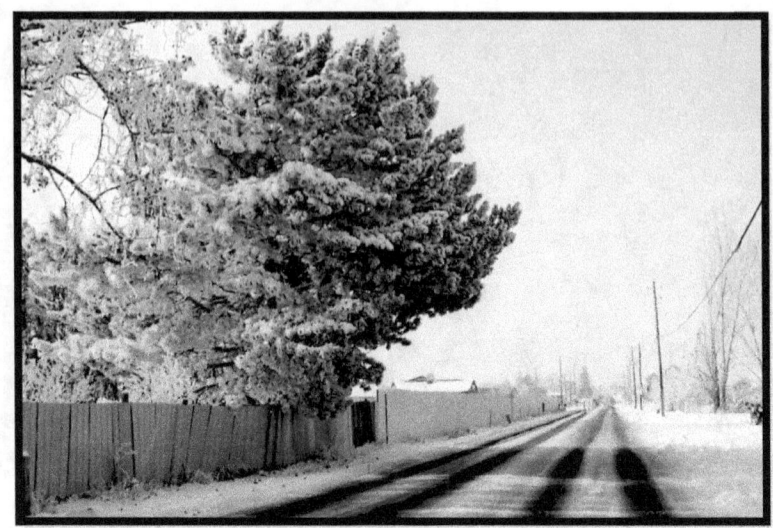

Long Road ahead greets those who travel.

Telephone Poles

Donkeys in an open field

while Sleeping in the morning Sun.

Rusty Tin Roof

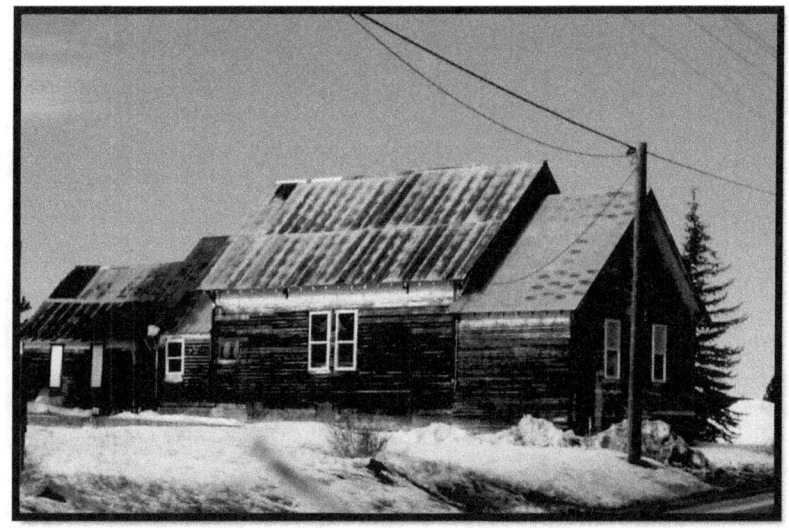

Settlers one lived in the house

with Rusty Tin Roofs off the main Road

leading into the Cascade Mountains.

Fisherman come and bring their Boats

as Hikers go Backpacking on new Trails unknown.

Horse and Plow

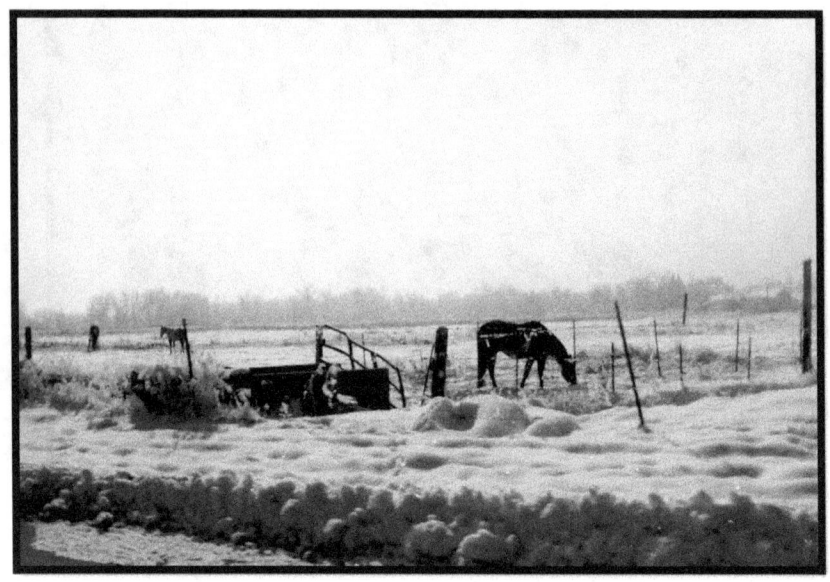

Dutch settlers come with their Horse Plows

in the break of a new day and Mothers hold their

Children reading stories in books.

The Fog lifts off in a new direction

as the Sun shines down on the Valley below.

Winter Morning

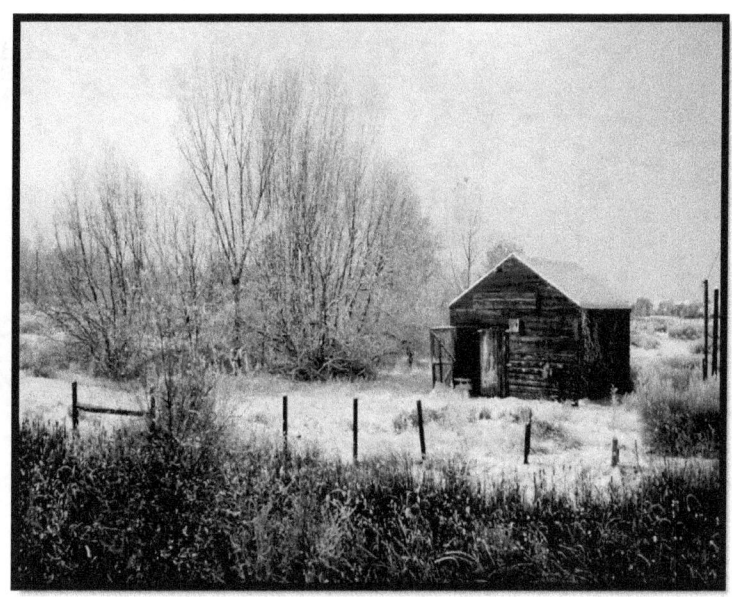

Open Door

Wooden Shed

Fence, Snow

Brush and Stark Trees.

Vintage Truck

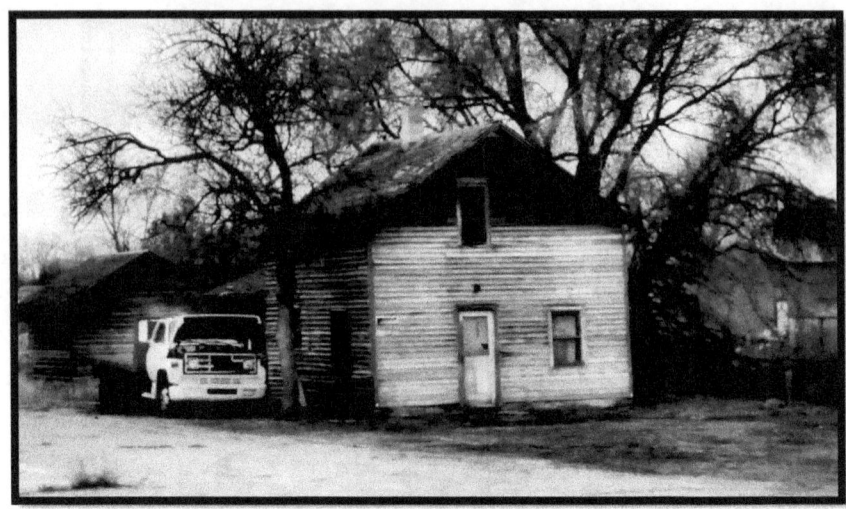

Rustic Barn

Vintage Truck

Stillness

Branches in Winter.

English Brick Cottage

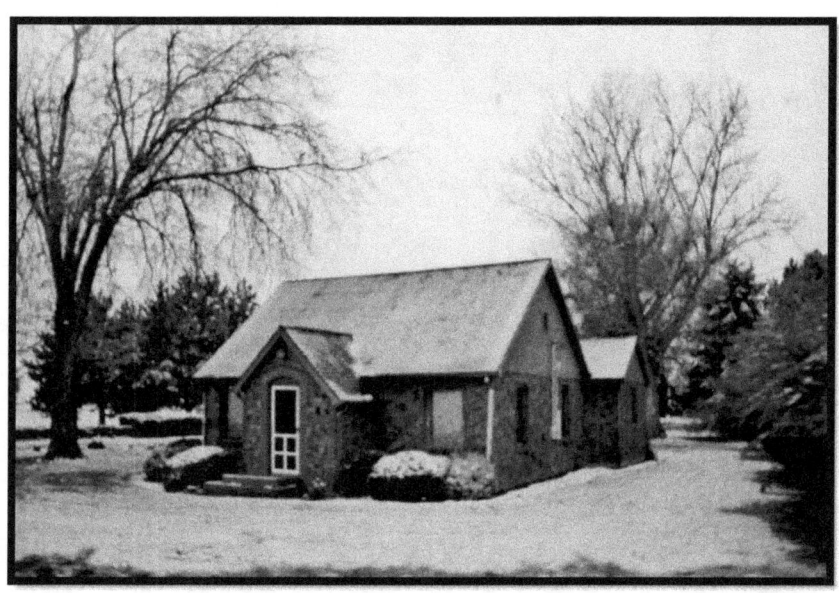

Snow covered Lawn

Winter Trees

Beauty of a English Cottage.

Rustic Barn in the Meadow

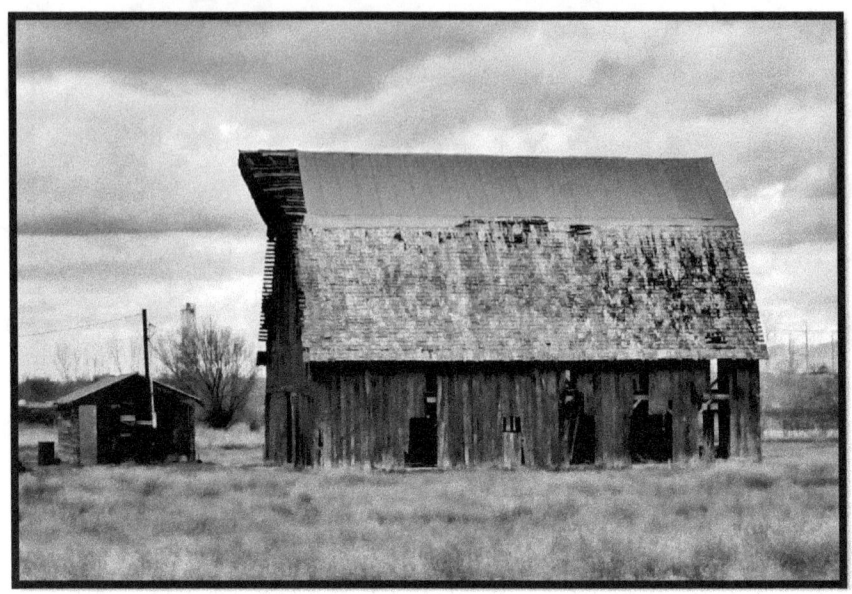

Cloudes

Rustic Barn

Meadows

Past Reflections.

Ranchers Farm

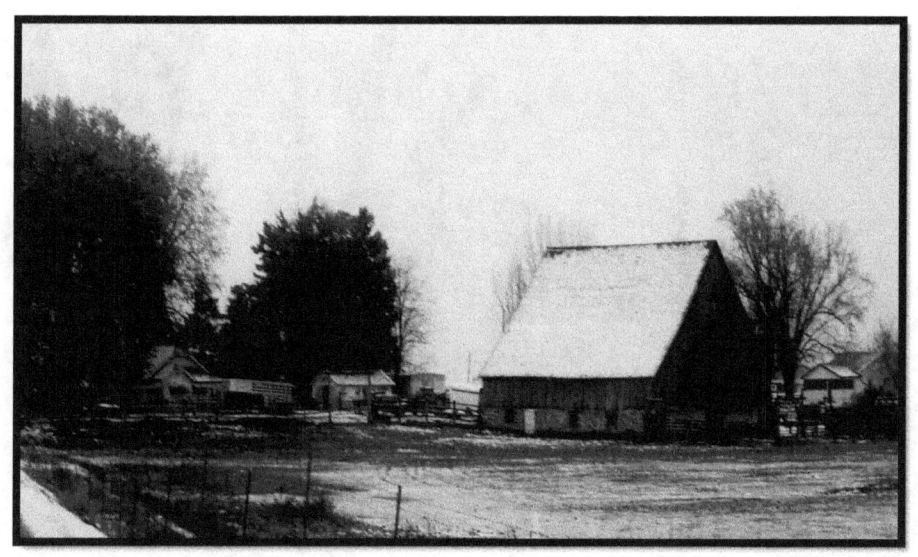

Snow coverd Barn

Ranch Life

in

Middleton

Past Reflections

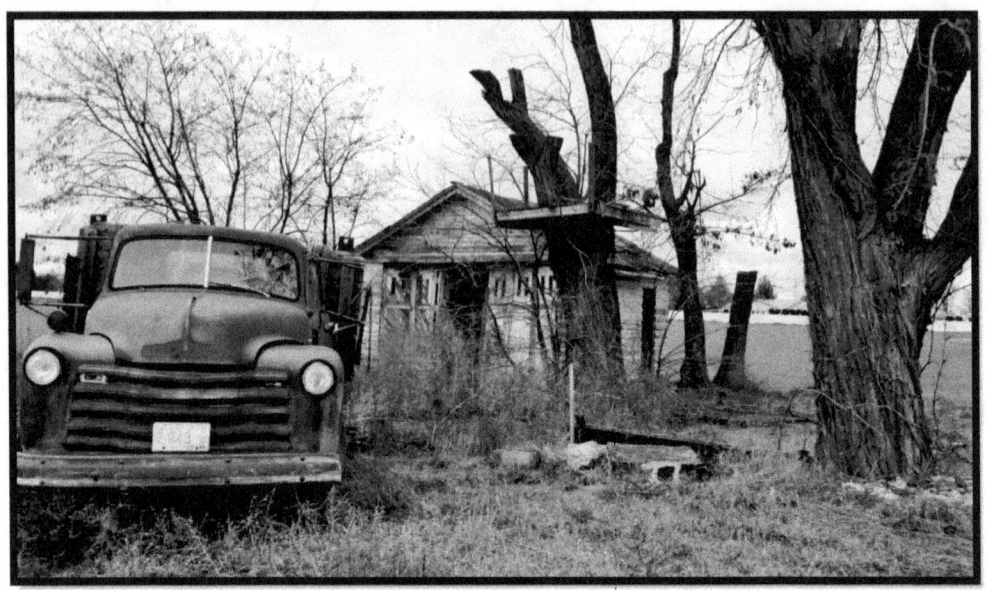

Vintage Truck

Shed

Tree Trunks

Farming land.

Snow Sleighing

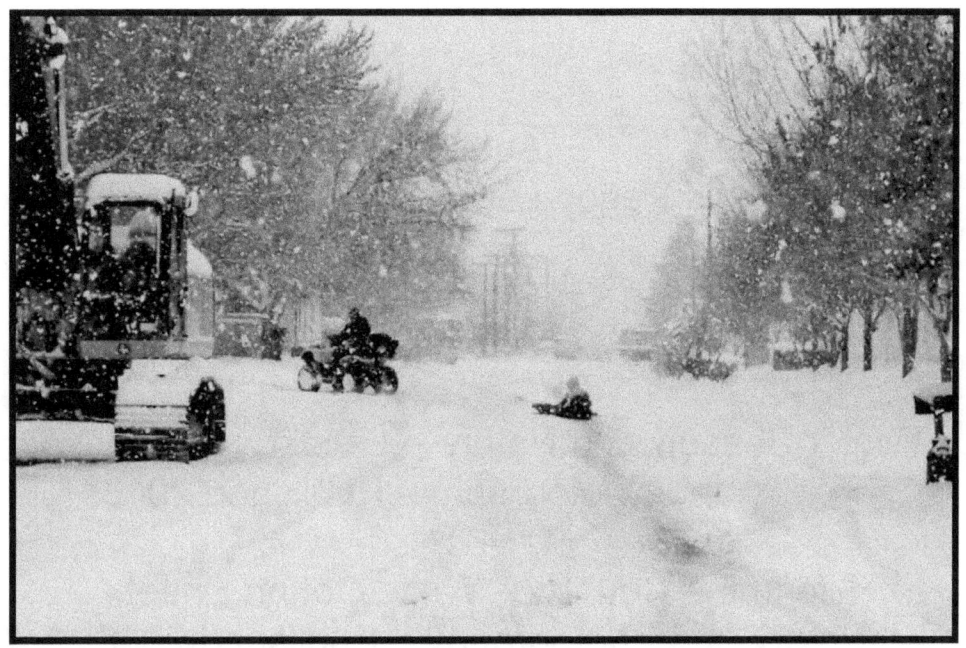

The Snow had just started coming down upon

arrival as one stood watching a Child being pulled

on a Sleigh during Winter Season. It was as pretty

and Picturesque as a Post-Card. Those days spent in

beautiful Idaho are a Treasure forever.

Literary Published Works

Author
Peggy Leyva Conley

Books

Winter Season with Nature – Landscape Scenes
Poetry and Photography - Published 2016

Life in the Country – White Cotton Sheets
Poetry and Photography – Published 2016

At the Heart of Aromatherapy – Nature Botanicals
Herbs – Soaps – Oils – Fragrance – Published 2016

The Transcendental Zen Garden
Poetry and Photography – Published 2016

Discography - Music

Passages of Time

(Classical: Film Music) - Released 2010

Canterbury Manor
(Classical: Chamber Music) – Released 2013

Ancient Garden of Knowledge
(Classical: Orchestral) – Released 2013

Midnight Telephone Blues
(Blues: Delta Style) - Released 2013

In the Face of Blues
(Acoustic Blues) – Released 2013

Mountain Blues
(Acoustic Blues) – Released 2013

Available on International Distribution

www.ingramcontent.com/pod-product-compliance
Lightning Source LLC
Chambersburg PA
CBHW080626190526
45169CB00009B/3300